CAMPAIGN 310

THE BAR KOKHBA WAR AD 132–136

The last Jewish revolt against Imperial Rome

LINDSAY POWELL

ILLUSTRATED BY PETER DENNIS

Series editor Marcus Cowper

First published in Great Britain in 2017 by Osprey Publishing,
PO Box 883, Oxford, OX1 9PL, UK
1385 Broadway, 5th Floor, New York, NY 10018, USA
E-mail: info@ospreypublishing.com

Osprey Publishing, part of Bloomsbury Publishing Plc

OSPREY is a trademark of Osprey Publishing, a division of Bloomsbury Publishing Plc.

A CIP catalogue record for this book is available from the British Library.

Print ISBN: 9781472817983
PDF e-book ISBN: 9781472817990
ePub e-book ISBN: 9781472818003
XML ISBN: 9781472822710

Index by Sharon Redmayne
Typeset in Myriad Pro and Sabon
Maps by Bounford.com
3D BEVs by The Black Spot
Originated by PDQ Media, Bungay, UK
Printed in China through China through World Print Ltd.

17 18 19 20 21 10 9 8 7 6 5 4 3 2 1

AUTHOR'S ACKNOWLEDGEMENTS & DEDICATION

For their kind help with this book, the author wishes to thank: Thortsen Opper of the British Museum, London; David Mevorah and the staff of Israel Museum, Jerusalem; Sarah Turel and Michal Bentovim of Eretz Israel Museum, Tel Aviv; Richard Beale of Roma Numismatics, London; Dale Tatro of Classical Numismatics Group, Lancaster, Pennsylvania; Carole Raddato of the *Following Hadrian* blog; Oved Abed and David and Ros Gutman in Austin, Texas; and finally Mark Judkins, my patient travel companion in Britain and Israel.

The book is dedicated to the men and women of the armed forces and police who put their lives at risk every day to defend our freedoms of speech, movement and association.

AUTHOR'S NOTE

The original written sources on which this book is based are variously written in Aramaic, Greek, Hebrew and Latin. Sometimes the meaning is obscure and one modern scholar's translation can be challenged by another. Often the texts are damaged or are no more than fragments so that whole words are missing, in which case experts try their best to fill in these lacunae using their skill and judgement. To this papyrological material, archaeology, epigraphy, numismatics, philology, military and religious studies can provide valuable insights, but these are also subject to interpretation. New discoveries and theories can (and do) overturn accepted ideas. Fully recognizing the challenges posed by the research material, this book represents the author's best attempt to build a coherent narrative of the events of AD 132–135/6 and readily accepts that it cannot be the last word on the Bar Kokhba War.

Several spellings of Hebrew names and places are possible in English. I have opted to spell Ben Koseba's moniker as Bar Kokhba (rather than Bar-Cochba, Bar Kochba, Bar Kokhva or Bar Kosba) where the 'kh' is pronounced 'ch' (as in the Scottish 'loch') and 'ba' as in the French 'va'. I use Rabbi Akiba in place of Akiva or Aquiba or Aquiva. For the city of Ben Koseba's last stand I have used Betar throughout (rather than Beitar, Bethar, Bethther, Beththera, Bithara or Bittîr), and Ein Gedi (rather than En-gedi or En Gedi).
The dating convention used throughout is the *Anno Domini* designation of BC/AD.

Translations of ancient texts are in the public domain: Cassius Dio's *Roman History* by E. Cary (1925) in the Loeb Classical Library; Eusebius' *Ecclesiastical History* by Kirsopp Lake (1926); the Old Testament books are from the King James Bible; the Midrash by Rev. Samuel Rapaport (1907); the Babylonian Talmud by Michael L. Rodkinson (1903–1918) and the Jerusalem Talmud by Dr Moses Schwab (1886). The translations of the Ben Koseba letters were taken from Yigael Yadin et al., *The Documents from the Bar-Kokhba Period in the Cave of Letters: Hebrew, Aramaic and Nabatean-Aramaic Papyri* (Israel Exploration Society, Israel, 1989–2002).

Unless otherwise accredited, all images are from the author's personal collection.

Osprey Publishing supports the Woodland Trust, the UK's leading woodland conservation charity. Between 2014 and 2018 our donations are being spent on their Centenary Woods project in the UK.

To find out more about our authors and books visit **www.ospreypublishing.com**. Here you will find extracts, author interviews, details of forthcoming events and the option to sign up for our newsletter.

ABBREVIATIONS

AE	*Année épigraphique*
CIL	*Corpus Inscriptionum Latinarum*
ILS	*Inscriptiones Latinae Selectae*
P. Mur	*The Documents from the Bar-Kokhba Period in the Cave of Letters*
P. Yadin	*The Documents from the Bar-Kokhba Period in the Cave of Letters*
RIB	*Roman Inscriptions of Britain*

GLOSSARY OF HEBREW WORDS

Av	Eleventh month of the Jewish civil calender, coinciding with parts of July and August.
Halakhah	Body of Jewish religious laws derived from the Written and Oral Torah.
Iyyar	Eighth month of the Jewish civil calender, coinciding with parts of April and May.
Midrash	Compendium of rabbinic commentaries of the Jewish Bible.
Mishnah	Collection of 'Oral Law' and rabbinic traditions which supplements, complements, clarifies and systematizes the commandments of the Torah.
Pesach	'Passover', a major eight-day festival celebrated in the early spring to commemorate the emancipation of the Israelites from slavery in Egypt.
Shavuot	Originally a harvest festival (held fifty days after the second day of Pesach), it now also commemorates the giving of the Torah by God to the Jews at Mount Sinai.
Sukkot	'Feast of Tabernacles', a major festival held in the autumn (beginning on the 15th day of *Tishri*) to commemorate the sheltering of the Israelites in the wilderness.
Talmud	Book of 613 commandments given by God to the Jews.
Tishri	First month of the Jewish civil calender, coinciding with parts of September and October.
Torah	Jewish 'Written Law', also known as the Five Books of Moses (Pentateuch) or Hebrew Bible (Tanakh), comprised of the first five books of the Old Testament.
Yom Kippur	'Day of Atonement', a high holiday falling ten days after the Jewish New Year (Rosh HaShanah) on the 10th of *Tishri*.

MEASURES

1 centimetre = 0.39 inches
1 metre = 3.28 feet
1 kilometre = 3,280.84 feet
1 Roman mile = 4,850 feet (1,478.3 metres)

CONTENTS

The Roman Empire, AD 132

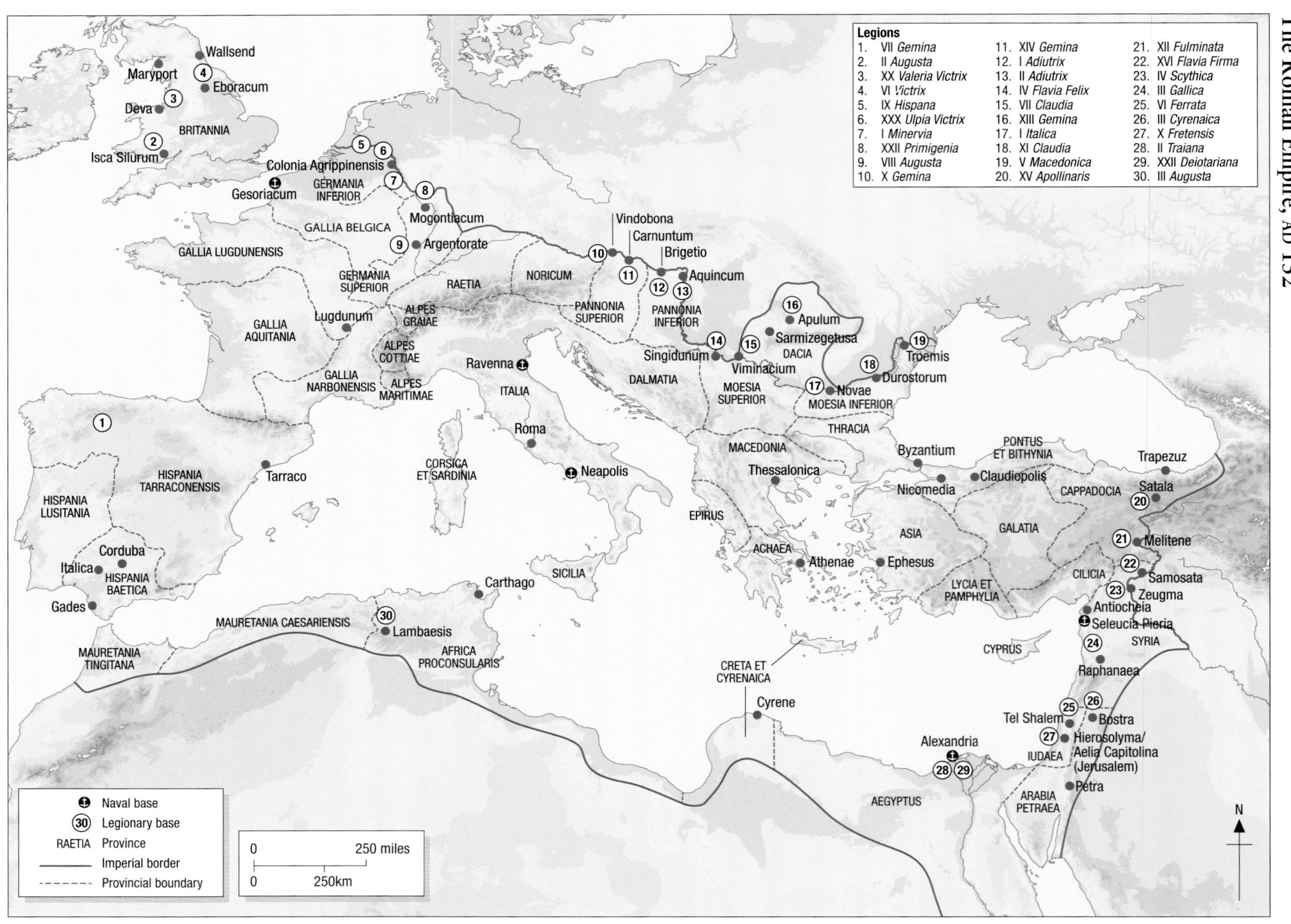

STRATEGIC SITUATION

BACKGROUND

In the spring of AD 130 Hadrian, commander-in-chief of the armed forces and 'first man' of the Roman world, arrived in Iudaea (Judaea). It was just one of several territories he was visiting on his tour of the provinces since leaving Rome two years before. Hadrian was in high spirits. He had inspected the border regions and army camps, raising morale and enforcing discipline in the military units stationed there. In towns and cities the crowds had welcomed him as *resitutor* (restorer) and celebrated athletic and gladiatorial games in his honour. Accompanying him was his male lover, a beautiful 19-year-old named Antinous from Bithynia, and a new-found source of happiness for the hard-working, vigorous older man. It seemed that the empire was enjoying a new golden age of peace and prosperity.

The people of Iudaea welcomed him too. As he travelled through the province the citizens of Tiberias, *colonia* Prima Flavia Augusta Caesarea (modern Caesarea), Salumias (Salem) and other towns received benefactions from him. Celebrating his visit, coins were struck bearing the legend 'For Augustus' Arrival in Iudaea' using his honorific title. The resident Jewish population also hoped for better relations with the emperor following decades of discontentment reaching back to the disastrous war in Iudaea of AD 66–74. Then, propelled by a national hope for redemption, radicalized Jews had seized Hierosolyma (or Yerushalayim, modern Jerusalem) to liberate it from Roman control, intending to install an independent government. The rebels

Hadrian toured the provinces, travelling great distances, often by sea, on an imperial galley powered by sail (when wind permitted) or by banks of oarsmen at other times. The legend, meaning 'Revered Good Luck', conveys both the good tidings of Hadrian's arrival and the happiness, prosperity and security he brought with him from Rome to the provinces. (Roma Numismatics, www.romanumismatics.com)

Hadrian's arrival (*adventus*) in Iudaea in AD 130 was a great state occasion. However, his ban on circumcision and plan for redeveloping Jerusalem (Hierosolyma) were considered extremely provocative to the Jewish community. (Classical Numismatics Group, www.cngcoins.com)

had minted coins boldly proclaiming 'Jerusalem [the] Holy' and 'Freedom [of] Zion'. The Roman army struck back. It besieged the ancient City of David aggrandized by Herod the Great and, in the summer of AD 70, retook it by force. The holy Second Temple was destroyed by fire. In a move calculated to cause maximum offence the holiest artefacts of Judaism were stripped from the Temple complex and paraded in Rome in triumph by the victorious commander Titus, son of emperor Vespasian (AD 69–79). The proceeds from the war spoils were used to build the *Amphitheatrum Flavium* (now known as the Colosseum), which was inaugurated by Titus as emperor (AD 79–81). Many of those not enslaved left Iudaea and joined the population of Jews in the diaspora. Tensions grew in these mixed communities. Exacerbating the situation, Vespasian imposed a punitive tax on all Jews (*fiscus Iudaicus*) irrespective of their location, which was later expanded to include a broader definition of Jewry by his other son Domitian when he subsequently became ruler (AD 81–96).

After Domitian died, the emperor Nerva (AD 96–98) removed the abuses of the Jewish Tax, but resentment among Jews against Rome for destroying the Temple and mutual hostility between them and their gentile neighbours drove many living in communities in the diaspora again to seek liberty and redemption. Their moment came when the new emperor Trajan launched his war against Parthia (Rome's long-time rival in the East), taking large numbers of troops with him. The emperor now distracted, in AD 115 Jews in Cyprus, Libya and Egypt turned upon symbols of Roman authority and its supporters.

On the island of Cyprus, one Artemion led Jewish insurgents in attacks on the gentile population. The Roman historian Cassius Dio claims 240,000 perished in the violence. Trajan dispatched Marcius Turbo (one of his best commanders) with infantry and cavalry aboard naval vessels to restore order. Men of *Legio* III *Cyrenaica* and *Legio* XXII *Deiotariana* as well as several auxiliary cohorts took part. A plan was even laid to dispatch the fleets from Misenum and Ravenna.

In Libya, Jewish rioters led by Andreas (or Lukuas) attacked their neighbours. They set alight public buildings, including the sanctuary of Apollo in Cyrene and of Asclepius at Balagrae. They toppled and smashed milestones along the road between Cyrene and its port, Apollonia, even ripping up the roadway itself to hinder any Roman troops arriving by sea from moving swiftly inland. Marcius Turbo and his expeditionary force may yet have landed and fought in Libya. To assist, Trajan sent C. Valerius Rufus, tribune of *Legio* II *Claudia* from Moesia Superior. Several of the agitators, however, travelled east to foment trouble in neighbouring Egypt.

In Egypt, riots between Greek-speaking Romans and Jews erupted in Alexandria and spread as far south as Thebes. The shrine of Nemesis near Alexandria was destroyed by Jewish rioters. The historian Appian (Appianus Alexandrinus) records in his *Roman History* how he narrowly escaped from angry Jewish forces, got lost at night while trying to find his ship, then at dawn next day found a trireme by accident and managed to reach Pelusium on the eastern side of the Nile Delta. (The ship he was supposed to board was captured by Jewish insurgents.) Aided by peasants, the Romans struck back. *Praefectus Aegypti* Rutilius Rufus personally led attacks upon the insurgents but, with contingents of the local army units away on campaign with Trajan, the remaining men of *Legio* III *Cyrenaica* and *Legio* XXII *Deiotariana* struggled to contain the situation.

Hadrian's deputy in the province of Iudaea was the *legatus Augusti pro praetore*, Q. Tineius Rufus. His home and office were in *colonia* Prima Flavia Augusta Caesarea. Originally built by Herod the Great, by AD 130 the *praetorium* was a complex covering some 12,000 square metres. Tineius' personal suite was on a promontory overlooking the sea. An inscription on a statue base confirms that Hadrian stayed here during his official visit. (Author's collection)

In Mesopotamia, which was within the Parthian Empire, the Jews banded together with other resistance groups to impede the advance of Trajan's invading army. The Roman commander-in-chief dispatched Lusius Quietus (a Moor of consular rank who had proved his worth at Nisibis and Edessa) to crush the insurgents beyond the Euphrates. There is a tantalizing reference to an *expeditio Iudaicae* (a military 'expedition in Iudaea') on an inscription found in Sardinia (*AE* 1929, 167), about which nothing more is known. He accomplished the task with such violence that the Midrash records the 'Kitos War' – or 'War of Quietus' – with sorrowful words.

Then, on 7 or 8 August AD 117, Trajan died unexpectedly. He was 64 years old.

His adopted successor, the 41-year-old Hadrian, inherited a world in turmoil. An experienced military leader in his own right, he immediately took command of the situation. He sent Marcius Turbo to Mauretania. Significantly, the new emperor appointed Lusius Quietus as military governor (*legatus Augusti pro praetore*) of Iudaea. (Hardly a year had passed when he was dead under mysterious circumstances.) Hadrian changed the status of the province of Iudaea from praetorian to consular. He replaced Quietus with L. Cossonius Gallus (consul of AD 116), based at the administrative capital of the province at Caesarea. He stepped up security measures. Hadrian doubled the military presence there to augment *Legio* X *Fretensis*, which had been encamped within Jerusalem's walls since AD 70. Initially *Legio* II *Traiana Firma* moved in (around AD 120). At a later date *Legio* VI *Ferrata* replaced

Supported on stone arches this aqueduct brought fresh water from the Shuni springs to *colonia* Caesarea. It was then distributed through underground pipes of clay or wood to public fountains, bathhouses and the homes of the wealthy in the city. (Author's collection)

it, establishing its camp at Tel Shalem in the Beth Shean Valley. Over the next decade the existing network of military roads was extended. Surviving milestones (all of them dated to AD 120 and 129–130) indicate that at least 12 roads were constructed by the army to facilitate troop movements in the densely populated regions with a recorded history of unrest. So far the strategy had worked; by the time of Hadrian's visit in AD 130 there had been no violent uprisings.

In AD 130 the city of Jerusalem was still in ruins 60 years after the great siege. The Temple itself had been destroyed by fire and the walls of the Temple Mount partially felled by Roman troops as punishment. Hadrian envisaged redeveloping the city as a new *colonia* (a city for veteran soldiers) with a temple of Jupiter Capitolinus at its centre. (Author's collection)

Bordered by Syria in the north, the Mediterranean Sea in the west and Arabia Petraea in the south and east, this minor Roman province encompassed the districts of Galilea, Samaria and Iudaea. In the north, Galilea (Galilee) was prosperous and Jews, early Christians and pagans mixed in the multicultural cities of Caesarea, Scythopolis (Beth Shean), Sepphoris (renamed Diocaesarea around the time of Hadrian's visit, modern Zippori) and Tiberias.

In the central region was Samaria with Flavia Neapolis (Shechem, modern Nablus) as its leading city. Its population was a mix of Samaritans, Jews, early Christians and pagans. Though their beliefs shared a common origin with the Jews in the tribal patriarch Abraham, the Samaritans claimed theirs to be the true religion of the ancient Israelites. Their temple was built on the holy hill of Gerizim, near Shechem, but it was destroyed in the 2nd century BC. There was a long-standing enmity between Jews and Samaritans, and the Samaritans often sided with enemies of the Jews.

Below Samaria the district of Iudaea was bordered in the east by the Dead Sea. On the coast, connected by a road, stood the cities of Ioppe (Yafo), Azotus (Ashdod), Ascalon (Ashkelon) and Gaza. Inland there was a major city at Hebron, many smaller towns – such as Betar, Bethlehem, Eleutheropolis (modern Beit Guvrin), Lydda (Lod) and Tekoa (El Khiam) – and numerous scattered villages and farms. Jerusalem was once its largest city, but in AD 130 it still lay largely in ruins. On the Dead Sea Ein Gedi thrived on account of its freshwater oasis, famed vineyards and valuable trade in balsam used in the perfume industry.

In terms of terrain Iudaea comprised quite distinct topographical zones. In the north there were high mountains (which could be snow capped in winter) formed of basalt and other igneous rocks, which cascaded eastwards down to the Sea of Galilee, a freshwater lake fed by the Jordan River that supplied abundant stocks of fish to the local population. In the central region the range of Judaean Hills, reaching up to 1,000m (3,280ft) in some places and made of hard chalk and dolomite, offered few natural resources except for areas of arable land and pasture used for grazing animals. The Judaean Desert descended south-eastwards from Jerusalem, ending in a deep escarpment that dropped steeply to the Dead Sea (fed by the Jordan River and underground springs). West of the Judaean Hills lay the Judaean Shephelah ('Judaean foothills'), an area of lowland formed of marl-covered soft chalk with pockets of fertile rolling plains. Naturally occurring in the landscape of Iudaea were caves. Farther south lay the dry expanse of the Negev Desert where vegetation was sparse.

Legio X *Fretensis* was encamped in or near the ruined city of Jerusalem. Its own construction needs required a brick and tile factory to be built. This brick bears the official stamp 'LEG X FR'. (Exhibit at the Israel Museum, Jerusalem. Author's collection)

Roman soldiers routinely patrolled the land and returned to barracks. After Quietus, Roman governors came and went. All the while, the Jews of Iudaea harboured their hope of national redemption and liberty. Since AD 70 the nature of Judaism had changed. The destruction of the Temple meant public worship and the sacrifices in Jerusalem specified in the Talmud could not now be carried out by the hereditary priests. Political power and judicial authority had shifted from the Sanhedrin (the assembly functioning as a supreme court consisting of up to 71 men appointed from every city in the Land of Israel) to the synagogues and prayer houses. There the emphasis was traditionally on studying and debating the Torah (see Glossary) under rabbis (teachers). Along with their students these teachers pored over the Torah for what it told of civil and criminal law, as well as the many religious statutes. The devout Jews now looked to their rabbis (instead of the Sanhedrin) to adjudicate in legal disputes and willingly accepted their rulings. Thus Rabbi Akiba was able to sentence an offender to pay a fine for uncovering a woman's head in the street, simply by the spiritual authority vested in his position.

CAUSES OF THE WAR

Some Jews may have even begun to believe that it might be possible to rebuild the Temple in Jerusalem. The Midrash and the Epistle of Barnabas (a Greek Christian text written between AD 70 and the early 2nd century) both appear to suggest that the Jews had received permission to rebuild it, though it is not entirely clear from other written records that that was the case. Hadrian, however, had an altogether different idea.

ABOVE LEFT
The Judaean Shephelah is a region of fertile farmland. In AD 130 (as it is today) it was suited to vineyards and unirrigated crops. To the east the terrain rises up to the Judaean Hills, which reach 800–1,000m (2,600–3,250ft) above sea level. In between the hills the broad vales are better suited to grazing animals. (Author's collection)

ABOVE RIGHT
The Judaean Desert lies to the south and east of Jerusalem. It ends in a steep escarpment that drops dramatically to the Dead Sea. This view looks north from the seashore to Kibbutz Ein Gedi – the lowest community on earth at some 400m (1,300ft) below sea level. (Author's collection)

While in the province, Hadrian trekked up along the road from Caesarea or Neapolis into the Judaean Hills, rising some 786m (2,577ft) above the level of the Mediterranean, to see Jerusalem for himself. 'Those who visited it could not believe it had ever been inhabited,' wrote Josephus (*Jewish War* 7.1.1) after the siege of AD 70. Archaeological evidence suggests that in the intervening 60 years the city was slowly recovering from the extensive war damage, in part through the activities of suppliers of goods and services to the resident legion; but Hadrian now envisaged completely rebuilding it in Roman fashion as a *colonia* for retired soldiers.

The city would have a radically new street plan and, among its amenities, it would feature a Temple of Jupiter Capitolinus on the site of the former Temple of the Jews' God. It would bear the name Aelia Capitolina in honour jointly of his family (*gens Aelia*) and the king of Roman gods. Hadrian's architect, a Greek-speaking man from Sinope in Pontus named Aquila, was commissioned to begin work. Hadrian may have intended no offence to the Jews. It was well known that he delighted in architecture and sponsored construction of new buildings wherever he went. The derelict city located in such a dramatic natural setting cried out to him for reconstruction. Work would begin without delay. Over the north gate a new inscription was unveiled. It read: 'To *Imperator* Caesar Traianus Hadrianus Augustus, son of the deified Traianus Parthicus, grandson of the deified Nerva, high priest, invested with Tribunician Power for the fourteenth time, Consul for the third time, Father of the Fatherland. [Dedicated by] *Legio* X *Fretensis*.'

This was a crushing blow to the local people, 'for the Jews deemed it intolerable that foreign races should be settled in their city and foreign religious rites planted there', writes Cassius Dio (*Roman History*, 69.12.2). It was now abundantly clear that there would be no rebuilding of the Temple. Indeed, according to the Mishnah a plough was driven over the Temple precinct. It was the quintessentially Roman purification rite conducted by a priest prior to digging the foundations of a new building – the Temple of Jupiter.

Even before Hadrian arrived in the province there had already been deep concern about his social policy. One of his recent edicts had been to ban the practice of circumcision. Hadrian's new directive put circumcision on a par with castration – a practice outlawed under the *Lex Cornelia* signed by Domitian and Nerva and deemed by the law as equivalent to murder. The Jews took particular offence to it. They believed the commandment to circumcise male children (*brit milah*) was given by God to Abraham in the Torah. It was one of the most ancient and defining practices of Judaism. Hadrian may, in fact, have not been specifically targeting Jews on religious grounds. Other subject peoples also engaged in the rite, among them the Arabs of Nabataea, Egyptians (at least high-ranking priests) and the Sarmatians. For Hadrian it was a barbaric custom, no less than a 'mutilation of the genitals' (Aelius Spartianus, *Life of Hadrian*, *Historia Augusta* 14.2). His personal sensibilities would not tolerate it. Nevertheless, despite protestations by Jews that it was a mortal blow to their faith and identity, the edict remained in force.

KING MESSIAH

His business in Iudaea concluded, Hadrian and his entourage departed – passing the hilltop city of Betar – on the road to Gaza bound for Arabia Petraea and Egypt. Whether or not he knew it, the emperor had left many Jews with deep feelings of outrage. To them it seemed that the Roman was deliberately singling out the Jewish people for harsh punishment. They were now highly motivated to establish a way to liberate their spiritual homeland from the hegemony of the Romans and to find a leader who would help them achieve it. Their yearning for an 'anointed one' – a *moshiah* (messiah) about whom they had read in their religious studies – had been awakened.

According to prevailing understanding, the *moshiah* referred to a future king of Israel, blessed by the God of the Jews. In the fourth book of the Torah it was written: 'I shall see him, but not now: I shall behold him, but not nigh: there shall come a Star out of Jacob, and a Sceptre shall rise out of Israel, and shall smite the corners of Moab, and destroy all the children of Sheth. And Edom shall be a possession, Seir also shall be a possession for his enemies; and Israel shall do valiantly' (*Numbers* 24:17–18). (Edom was widely construed at the time to mean Rome.)

In the *Book of Ezekiel*, God approaches the prophet exiled in Babylon and says to him: 'And I will set up one shepherd over them, and he shall feed them, *even* my servant David; he shall feed them, and he shall be their

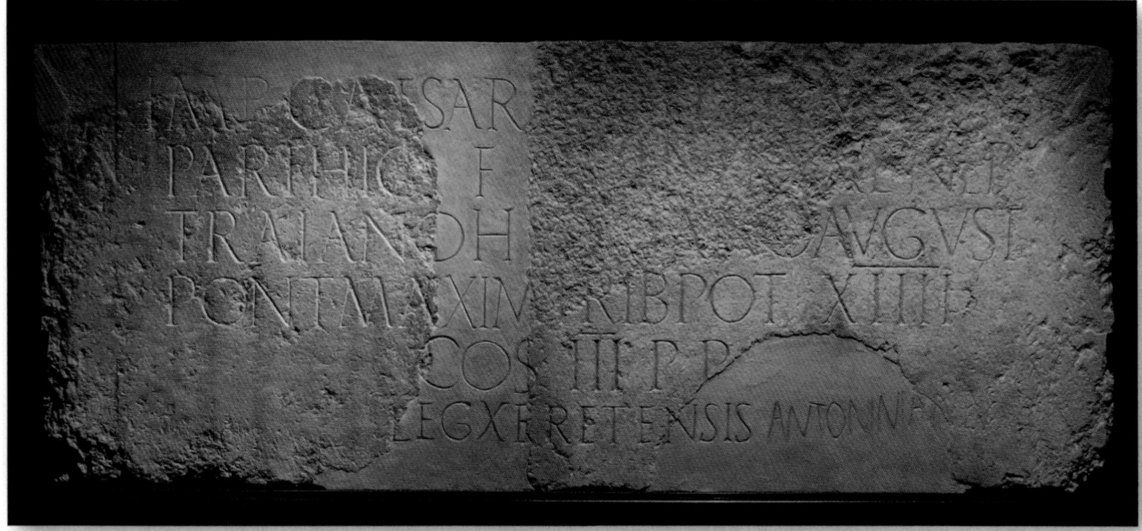

Before Hadrian left Jerusalem in AD 130 an inscription mounted over the north gate of the city may have been dedicated in his honour. Two segments of it have been discovered. The additional legionary title *Antoniniana* was carved several years later. (Exhibit at the Israel Museum, Jerusalem. Author's collection)

shepherd. And I the Lord will be their God, and my servant David a prince among them' (*Book of Ezekiel* 34:23–24). Further:

> Behold, I will take the children of Israel from among the heathen, whither they be gone, and will gather them on every side, and bring them into their own land: And I will make them one nation in the land upon the mountains of Israel; and one king shall be king to them all: and they shall be no more two nations, neither shall they be divided into two kingdoms any more at all: Neither shall they defile themselves any more with their idols, nor with their detestable things, nor with any of their transgressions: but I will save them out of all their dwelling places, wherein they have sinned, and will cleanse them: so shall they be my people, and I will be their God. (*Book of Ezekiel* 37:21–23)

As described in the apocalyptic Jewish literature, such as 'The Vision of the Seventy Shepherds' (*Book of Enoch* 85–90), the messiah would be a fierce warrior who would kill the unjust leader of the pagan world by his own hand, destroy his army and rid Jersualem of the impious heathen. Anointed with holy oil, this 'king messiah' would bring the scattered Jews back into the Land of Israel and unite them in a kingdom of peace and justice. He would build the Third Temple, father a male heir, and cause other great things to happen in a Messianic Age. Born of the earth (rather than sent from Heaven) this *moshiah* would be descended from the royal line of David (the biblical king who was both a successful war leader and a writer of psalms). A key line in one religious text read: 'Behold, O Lord, and raise up unto them their king, the son of David, at the time known to you, O God, in order that he may reign over Israel your servant' (*Psalms of Solomon* 17:21).

Some anticipated the imminent end of times, heralding the arrival of the prophesied messiah. According to the Babylonian Talmud, the prophet Elijah (9th century BC) had 'said to Rab Judah, the brother of Rabbi Salia the pious: "The world shall exist not less than eighty-five jubilees, and in the last jubilee the son of David will come"' (*Sanhedrin* 97b).

One man did emerge, who many believed fitted the description of the king messiah. His name was Shim'on ben Koseba. His moment had come.

Hadrian's visit had coincided with the appointment of Q. Tineius Rufus as his new *legatus Augusti pro praetore* in the province of Iudaea. It would fall to Rufus to deal with the consequences of his superior's unpopular policy decisions.

His visit to Iudaea completed, Hadrian and his entourage continued to Egypt. It would be a fateful trip. His young male lover, Antinous, drowned in the Nile on 30 October that same year. He was deified soon after and a cult centre was established at Antinoopolis close to the place of his death. (Roma Numismatics, www.romanumismatics.com)

CHRONOLOGY

All dates are AD

44	Death of Herodes Agrippa I, King of Iudaea; Romans impose control of Iudaea, riots in major cities.
66–74	First Jewish War.
66	Jewish rebels seize control of Hierosolyma.
70	Siege of Hierosolyma by T. Flavius (son of T. Flavius Vespasianus)
August	Destruction of the Second Temple, Hierosolyma (9 *Av*).
71	Triumph of T. Flavius Vespasianus for victory in the Jewish War.
73	Siege of Masada by Flavius Silva.
74	Romans capture Masada.
80	Opening of the *Amphitheatrum Flavium* (Colosseum) paid for from proceeds of the sale of spoils of the Jewish War.
98	
28 January	Death of Nerva.
February	Accession of M. Ulpius Traianus (Trajan) as emperor.
115–117	Revolt of the Jewish diaspora (Cyprus, Egypt, Libya, Iudaea, Mesopotamia), also known as the Kitos War.
116	Rutilius Rufus leads counterinsurgency against Jewish populations of Egypt.
	To quell Jewish insurrections, Trajan sends Q. Marcius Turbo to Egypt, C. Valerius Rufus to Cyprus and Lusius Quietus to Mesopotamia.
117	Hadrian in Antiocheia, Syria as *legatus Augusti pro praetore*.
7 or 8 August	Trajan adopts Hadrian. Death of Trajan at Selinus, Cilicia.
9 August	News of Trajan's death reaches Hadrian at Antiocheia.
11 August	Hadrian acclaimed as *imperator* for the first time at Antiocheia.
	Q. Marcius Turbo sent by Hadrian to Mauretania to quell local rebellion.
	Lusius Quietus in Iudaea as *legatus Augusti pro praetore*.
	Second legion (VI *Ferrata*) transferred to garrison Iudaea.
	Jewish partisans begin stockpiling weapons and converting caves into hiding places and storage.
118	
9 July	Hadrian arrives in Rome.
	Trajan's conquests in Assyria, Mesopotamia and Parthia abandoned, except Armenia.
	Death of Lusius Quietus?
119	Hadrian tours Campania.
Aug–Oct	M. Paccius Gargilius Antiquus as suffect consul.
120	L. Cossonius Gallus in Iudaea as *legatus Augusti pro praetore*.
	Hadrian in Rome.
May–June	C. Publicius Marcellus as suffect consul in Rome.
	Legionary vexillations begin improving the road network of Iudaea; establishment of base at Caparcotna in Iudaea for *Legio* VI *Ferrata*.

121–125	Hadrian's first tour of the Roman provinces.
121	Hadrian visits Tres Galliae, Germania Superior, Raetia, Noricum.
122	Hadrian visits Germania Inferior, Britannia (Londinium, Vindolanda, commissions the Wall), Tres Galliae, Hispania Tarraconensis (Tarraco).
	Second Moorish Revolt.
	M. Paccius Gargilius Antiquus in Syria as *legatus Augusti pro praetore.*
123	Hadrian visits Mauretania (?), Africa (?), Libya, Cyrene, Crete, Syria, the Euphrates frontier (Melitene), Pontus, Bithynia (meets Antinous for the first time), Asia.
124	Hadrian visits Thracia, Asia, Athens, Eleusis, Achaea.
	Q. Tineius Rufus in Thracia as *legatus Augusti pro praetore.*
125	Hadrian visits Achaea, Sicily; returns to Rome.
126	Hadrian in Rome.
127	Hadrian in Rome.
May–Sept	Q. Tineius Rufus as suffect consul in Rome.
Oct–Dec	Sex. Iulius Severus as suffect consul in Rome.
128–132	Hadrian's second tour of the Roman provinces.
128	Hadrian visits Africa, Rome, Athens.
Winter	Hadrian in Athens.
129	Hadrian visits Asia, Pamphylia, Phrygia, Pisidia, Cilicia, Syria, Commagene (Samosata), Cappadoceia, Pontus, Syria (Antiocheia).
	C. Publicius Marcellus in Syria as *legatus Augusti pro praetore*
130	Q. Tineius Rufus in Iudaea as *legatus Augusti pro praetore.*
	T. Haterius Nepos in Arabia Petraea in Iudaea as *legatus Augusti pro praetore.*
	Hadrian visits Iudaea (Caesarea, Scythopolis (?), founds *colonia* Aelia Capitolina on site of former Hierosolyma), Arabia Petraea, Egypt.
30 October	Hadrian's lover Antinous drowns in the Nile River; City of Antinoopolis founded.
131	Sex. Iulius Severus in Britannia as *legatus Augusti pro praetore.*
	Hadrian visits Syria, Asia.
Winter	Hadrian in Athens.
132–135	Second Jewish War led by Shim'on ben Koseba.
132	Hadrian in Rome.
Summer	Jewish partisans led by Shim'on ben Koseba at Herodium seize villages and towns throughout Iudaea (except Jerusalem); attack on Roman camp at Tel Shalem (?)
	Rabbi Akiba declares Shim'on ben Koseba to be Bar Kokhba ('son of a star') (?)
19 August	Last dated letter of Babatha of Maoza (found in the 'Cave of Letters', Nahal Hever)
	Trial and execution of Rabbi Akiba in Caesaraea (?)
133	C. Publicius Marcellus arrives in Iudaea with vexillations from Syria.
	T. Haterius Nepos arrives in Iudaea with vexillations from Arabia Petraea Shim'on ben Koseba at Herodium.
134	Q. Lollius Urbicus arrives in Iudaea as *legatus imperatoris Hadriani in expeditione Iudaica* with vexillations from Pannonia Superior.

	Sex. Iulius Severus arrives in Iudaea with vexillations from Britannia and Moesia Inferior
May–Sept	T. Haterius Nepos as suffect consul in Rome.
Winter	Hadrian in Rome.
	Jews from the Roman province of Arabia Petraea, Galilee and Transjordan find refuge in caves in the Judaean Desert.
135	Hadrian in Rome.
	Shim'on ben Koseba chastises the militia leaders of Tekoa.
May–Sept	Q. Lollius Urbicus as suffect consul in Rome.
Spring	Siege of Betar; Shim'on ben Koseba at Betar.
4 August	Fall of Betar, capture and slaughter of all inhabitants (9 *Av*); death of Eleazar of Modi'in and Shim'on ben Koseba.
Autumn	Jewish survivors of the revolt flee to caves in the Judaean Desert.
	Romans blockade refuge caves near Ein Gedi.
	Iudaea incorporated into Syria as Syria-Palaestina.
	Dedication of Temple of Venus et Roma in Rome.
136	Hadrian in Rome.
	Hadrian acclaimed *imperator* for second time.
	Triumphal ornaments awarded to Sex. Iulius Severus (celebrated at Aequum), C. Publicius Marcellus (Aquileia) and T. Haterius Nepos (Fulginiae).
	Triumphal arch erected at Tel Shalem, base of *Legio* VI *Ferrata* in Iudaea. Hadrian adopts L. Ceionius Commodus (L. Aelius Caesar).
	Mopping-up operations continue across Iudaea; blockade of refuge caves at Ein Gedi.
	Sex. Iulius Severus in Syria as *legatus Augusti pro praetore*.
Winter	End of blockade of refuge caves.
137	Hadrian in Rome.
138	
1 January	Death of L. Aelius Caesar.
25 February	Hadrian adopts T. Aurelius Fulvus Antoninus (acting as joint emperor).
10 July	Death of Hadrian.
11 July	Accession of T. Fulvus Aelius Hadrianus Antoninus Augustus Pius.
139	Completion of Hadrian's Mausoleum, Rome.
145	Dedication of Temple of *Divus* Hadrianus in the *Campus Martius*, Rome by Antoninus Pius.
1948	
14 May	Foundation of the State of Israel with its capital at Jerusalem.
1982	
11 May	(*Lag B'Omer*) Ceremonial burial of bones from the Cave of Horrors and Cave of Letters at Nahal Hever.
2015	
22 December	*Hadrian: An Emperor Cast in Bronze* exhibition opens at Israel Museum, Jerusalem.
2016	
20 Feb–18 June	*Bar Kokhba: Historical Memory and the Myth of Heroism* exhibition at Eretz Israel Museum, Tel Aviv.
27 June	*Hadrian: An Emperor Cast in Bronze* exhibition closes at Israel Museum, Jerusalem.

OPPOSING COMMANDERS

THE JEWS AND THEIR ALLIES

The military leader of the Jewish revolution was **Shim'on ben Koseba** (*c.* AD 95–135). He was an only son and he may have been the nephew of Rabbi Eleazar of Modi'in. The patronymic may indicate that a man named Koseba was his father, or that he came from a place of the same name (perhaps Kirbet Kosiba, a village or town north-west of Hebron, Palestine). Nothing is recorded of his upbringing, beyond that he was raised a Jew. At some point in his life he acquired the title to land near Herodium. He was likely married. The medieval Jewish sources mention that he had a son named Rufus. Another states that he was descended from the royal House of David – a crucial claim if he was to be seen as the *moshiah*.

Ben Koseba appears in the secular and religious texts fully formed as a rebel leader. He consciously presented himself as a leader who could be perceived by his followers as messianic. The formal title he adopted for himself was 'Prince (or President) Over Israel' (*Nasi' Yisra'el*), which was sometimes used on correspondence (e.g. *P. Yadin* 45). The title both established his claim to royalty and emphasized the national dimension of his political aspiration, which was grounded in a religious hope to found a land of the Jews.

To the Romans he was 'murderous and bandit-like' (Eusebius, *Church History* 4.6.2). In contrast the Jewish religious writings portray him as a man of extraordinary physical strength: it was said he was able to withstand the shock of a Roman ballista ball on his knee and to lob it back at the enemy; and he could kill a man with a single kick of his foot. A leader able to perform such great feats was called a *gibbor*, and, although Ben Koseba is not specifically called this anywhere in the Jewish texts, the implication was there nevertheless. (The biblical Samson, Judah Maccabee and his brothers were renowned *gibborim*). A seemingly unbreakable spirit drove this fearless warrior leader of his troops in the battle against the gentile foe. Yet the same accounts show this hero also as arrogant, quick-tempered and sometimes overconfident.

Ben Koseba's own writings reveal that he could be a tough, uncompromising and harsh leader. He demanded complete obedience from his subordinates. Indeed, he might even be described as a micro-manager in the way he detailed missions and rebuked those who failed to carry them out, even using sarcasm to make his point. Understandably he would have believed

Able to read and write, Shim'on ben Koseba, 'Prince of Israel', wrote constantly to his deputies, issuing orders and reprimands for failure to comply. This stamp – designed by Meir Eshel and issued by the Israel Post Office in December 2008 – reproduces a letter he wrote to Yeshua ben Galgula. The name 'Koseba' is written in Hebrew in Jewish-Aramaic script on the *se-tenant* tab. A devout Jew, it is believed that Hebrew became the official language of Israel by order of Ben Koseba. (Author's collection)

that compliance with his plan was crucial to its ultimate success. Yet the extensive preparations for the war suggest he was a master of military strategy and a good tactical planner. Where he learned the arts of war is unknown. It may have come from having lived among bandits. He appears to have been a charismatic leader too. One surviving letter addresses him as 'beloved father', though this could have been a formality. He himself referred to his fellow fighters as 'brothers'.

Interpreting religious texts, Rabbi Akiba recognized Shim'on ben Koseba as the long-awaited King Messiah (*moshiah*). He declared him to be the 'Bar Kokhba', 'Son of a Star', interpreting *Numbers* 24:17. This street sign in Jerusalem reads: 'Of the greatest Tannaim and Mishnah scholars, [he] taught 24,000 students. [One] Of the ten martyrs.' (Author's collection)

He was a literate man, educated in Jewish scripture and his letters use Talmudic terminology, but the degree to which his knowledge extended beyond that canon – to Greek or Latin literature – is not known. He mandated that Hebrew (the language of the Israelites and their ancestors) be the national language of the new Israel. Above all Ben Koseba was a devout Jew. Even in the midst of war he scrupulously kept the Sabbath for rest and rejoicing; he observed the holy days, such as Pesach and Sukkot, and traditional rituals of his ancient faith. His sincere piety and zeal attracted the attention of one of the pre-eminent religious leaders of the time.

Ben Koseba's armour-bearer (*nose kelav*) was **Akiba ben Yosef** (*c.* AD 50–132 or 137), known as Rabbi Akiba. He was born in Diospolis (Lydda, modern Lod) and spent his early life as a poor, illiterate shepherd. At his wife's urging, he went on to study under the eminent Mishnaic sage Eliezer ben Hyrcanus (*c.* AD 45–117), whom he regarded as 'rabbi'. By age 47 Akiba had established a reputation of his own as a great scholar of the Jewish law and founded a school at Beneberak (located just outside Jaffa) that attracted many students. Among his protégés was Rabbi Shim'on bar Yochai. In AD 95–96 Akiba was in Rome and by 110 had been to Nehardea, visiting many Jewish communities on his travels. It seems unlikely that he took part in any of the anti-Roman uprisings in the diaspora or Galilee. Far from being an arrogant man or political agitator he was modest by nature, given to acts of kindness towards the sick and needy. He was also intellectually gifted, contributing to the systematic organization of the Halakhah and the means to study them. The Talmud compares him to Moses, which is the highest compliment in Jewish literature. Akiba was one of the greatest of the first rabbis (*tannaim*) whose words are recorded in the Midrash and Mishnah.

Ben Koseba had a deputy. He is presumed to be the man whose name, **Eleazar the Priest**, appears on several coins after AD 132. Three candidates are suggested for this individual: Eleazar of Modi'in (El'azar HaModai); Eleazar ben Azariah; and Eleazar ben Harsom. Tantalizingly, in the rabbinic sources Rabbi Eleazar of Modi'in is mentioned as the uncle of Ben Koseba. (It has been suggested, however, that the Eleazar cited on the coinage was not a living person at all, but was actually a reference to Eleazar the Priest, son of Aaron from the time of Joshua.) The Jerusalem Talmud calls him 'the arm of all Israel' and 'their right eye' (Midrash Rabbah, *Lamentations* 2.2.4). The dual partnership between the warrior prince and the priest in the rebel administration was highly significant. It aligned the political and military aims of the messianic leader and his mission with the duty of serving the Hebrew god. Prayer and the sword would both be needed in this new Jewish state.

Several military commanders appointed by Ben Koseba are known by name from his letters, several examples of which were found in the Judaean Desert in modern times. Yeshua ben Galgula of the village Bet Bazi commanded the garrison of the nearby Herodium. Three men (Yehonathan bar Be'ayan, Masabala ben Shim'on of Tekoa and Eleazar ben Hitah) jointly commanded the region of Ein Gedi and reported to one Elisha. Shim'on ben Mahanim controlled an area of uncertain identity, which may be the Machaerus region of Transjordan or the Zif region in the south Hebron hills. Yehudah ben Manasseh served in Kiryat Arbaya. They each worked alongside civilian administrators (*parnasim*) appointed by Ben Koseba. From a lead weight found at Horbat 'Alim the *parnas* is known to have been Shim'on Dasoi.

These men would strive to establish a free Jewish nation and defend it with their lives from the inevitable onslaught of the Roman army.

THE ROMANS AND THEIR ALLIES

Imp. Caesar Traianus Hadrianus Augustus (24 January AD 76 to 10 July AD 138) was commander-in-chief (*imperator*) of all Roman military forces. He was born P. Aelius Hadrianus to an affluent family living in Baetica in the Iberian Peninsula. When his parents died unexpectedly in AD 85 or 86 the 10-year-old boy became ward of M. Ulpius Traianus, the son of Hadrian's maternal great-uncle and a rising star in the military. This connection would be crucial to his advancement through the Roman career ladder (*cursus publicus*), which combined military and civilian positions of increasing responsibility designed to expose a young man to a wide variety of aspects of public service in the Empire that might culminate in his election to one of the two annually appointed consuls (or their suffects).

Having worked in his late teens as a junior magistrate, Hadrian was appointed to his first army posting at age 20 as one of a team of military tribunes with *Legio* II *Adiutrix* (*c.* AD 94–95) based in Pannonia at Aquincum (modern Budapest) on the Danube River. Trajan was probably the governor (*legatus Augusti pro praetore*) of the province and it is likely on account of his influence that Hadrian secured the position. During his time with the unit, Hadrian made the acquaintance of Q. Marcius Turbo, then a centurion, with whom he struck up a friendship. In February AD 98 Trajan became emperor. Still as *tribunus militum*, Hadrian then transferred to V *Macedonica* stationed at Oescus in Moesia Inferior before moving (AD 97–98) to XXII *Primigenia* in Mogontiacum (modern Mainz) on the Rhine in Germania Superior.

Moving to Rome he served as one of the 20 *quaestores* responsible for public finance, a post which granted him entry to the Senate. As one of the nominees of the emperor he read aloud the official communications of Trajan, who was away fighting the First Dacian War (AD 101–102). While doing so he 'provoked a laugh by his somewhat provincial accent' (Aelius Spartianus, *Life of Hadrian* 3.1). Embarrassed by the episode he devoted time and effort to improving his speech 'until he attained the utmost proficiency and fluency'. He was later elected as Tribune of the Plebs (*tribunus Plebis*, AD 102) and then, with the emperor back in Rome, served as *praetor* (105) responsible for administering law and the courts.

Hadrian was a hard-working and restless commander-in-chief, travelling the Roman world to inspect the frontiers, and enforcing discipline among the troops guarding them. With a passion for art and architecture his generosity also benefited the civilian communities he visited. This coin declares him to be 'Restoration of Africa'. His plans for Jerusalem were in the same vein. (Roma Numismatics, www.romanumismatics.com)

He returned to army life when Trajan appointed him *legatus legionis* of I *Minervia Pia Fidelis* (AD 105–106), at the time on active service in the final stages of the Second Dacian War. Immediately following this, Trajan assigned him to Pannonia Inferior as *legatus Augusti pro praetore* (AD 106–108). There 'he held the Sarmatians in check, maintained discipline among the soldiers, and restrained the procurators, who were overstepping too freely the bounds of their power' (Aelius Spartianus, *Life of Hadrian* 3.9).

Hadrian returned to Rome in AD 108 to serve as a suffect consul from May to August. He went to Athens where he served as archon (AD 112–113) and developed a deep love of Greek culture that would stay with him for the rest of his life. He also began the practice of wearing a beard, at a time when the fashion was to be clean-shaven. Hadrian had developed into 'a pleasant man to meet and he possessed a certain charm' (Cassius Dio, *Roman History* 69.2.6[2]).

By AD 113 Hadrian was on his way to Syria while Trajan made preparations for a war against Parthia. The campaign against the Romans' arch-nemesis proved successful, but within the empire there was unrest across the Jewish diaspora and the East. It was while in Antiocheia (modern Antakya) that Hadrian received news of Trajan's death and that he had been adopted as his son. Hadrian succeeded him on 11 August AD 117 and was acclaimed *imperator* by the assembled troops. He was only the second non-Italian to rule (Trajan having been the first).

The sum of his military experience led Hadrian to believe that imperial expansion was folly. Now commander-in-chief he implemented a policy of containment, quickly abandoning most of his predecessor's conquests (except Armenia and Dacia). He undertook a series of tours of the provinces to inspect the frontiers and installations. He enforced discipline among the troops wherever he went. His letters and speeches reveal Hadrian to have been a somewhat reticent man and always working. He was very proud of his knowledge of military matters and was sure that he would notice any irregularity in a review of the troops. He made a point of eating the same food as the regular troops, going on their route marches, getting to know the soldiers personally and visiting them when they were sick.

By AD 132 he had been commander-in-chief for 15 years. Crucial to the efficient running of the empire were the propraetorian legates he personally appointed to the provinces. These direct reports were not career military but (like himself) men who had risen through the *cursus publicus*.

Hadrian had known – and come to trust – them personally during his own rise to prominence, and upon them he would now rely to prosecute the *Bellum Iudaicum*.

At the outbreak of the insurgency **Q. Tineius Rufus** (between *c.* AD 80 and 131) was in Iudaea as *legatus Augusti pro praetore*. His earlier career is entirely lost to us, but he almost certainly followed the standard template of the *cursus publicus*. He rose to suffect consul for May to September AD 127. His appointment as governor three years later confirms the change in status of Iudaea to a consular province. Based in *colonia* Prima Flavia Augusta Caesarensis (Caesarea), he would have been in Iudaea when Hadrian made his state visit the same year. He had command of two legions, VI *Ferrata* and X *Fretensis*.

In charge of neighbouring Syria to the north, was *Legatus Augusti Pro Praetore* **C. Quinctius Certus Publicius Marcellus**, (*c.* AD 75 to after 136). After a career of increasing responsibilities, Marcellus achieved the suffect consulship for May to June of AD 120. He assumed his governorship of Syria in AD 129 – certainly by the second half of 131. From his office at Antiocheia, Publicius Marcellus had command of three legions (III *Gallica,* IIII *Scythica* and XVI *Flavia Firma*) and several cohorts of auxiliaries. While he was away his deputy, Ti. Severus (the legate of *Legio* IIII *Scythica*), took charge of Syria.

Also in Syria was **Sex. Cornelius Dexter** (*c.* AD 70 to after 136). A native of Mauretania Caesariensis, his career is recorded on an inscription (*CIL* VIII, 8934 = *ILS* 1400) found at *colonia* Saldae (modern Béjaïa in Kabylia, eastern Algeria). Three times he was prefect of a military workshop (*praefectus fabrum*), during which time he would have commanded teams of skilled engineers (*fabri*). The *fabri* repaired damaged armour, constructed and maintained the artillery and siege equipment, built bridges and superintended mining operations. The office of *praefectus fabrum* was one of the highest trust and importance. Among his other assignments was a stint as *praefectus* of *Cohors* V *Raetorum*, an auxiliary cohort originally formed of recruits from Raetia (modern Austria) but had long since seen service in other parts of the Roman world. Around AD 129–130 he served as *tribunus militum* with *Legio* VIII *Augusta* based at Argentorate (Strasbourg) in Germania Superior. Thereafter, as prefect of *Ala Augustae Geminae*, he commanded an *ala quinquagenaria* – a unit of 500 cavalry – stationed in Cappadocia. In AD 132 Cornelius Dexter may have still been in that position, but was later appointed equestrian prefect of the navy in Syria (*Praefectus Classis Syriacae*), almost certainly by Hadrian himself.

To the south was **T. Haterius Nepos** (*c.* AD 90 to after 136). In AD 132 he was *legatus Augusti pro praetore* of Arabia Petraea (the territory annexed by Trajan in AD 105–106). He had one legion (III *Cyrenaica*) under his command. He was a native of Fulginiae (modern Foligno), according to the find of an inscription (*CIL* XI, 5212 = *ILS* 1058). In Egypt **T. Flavius Titianus**, who had been *praefectus Aegypti* since AD 126, had command of two legions (II *Traiana Fortis* and XXII *Deiotariana*).

Stationed on the Danube River was **Q. Lollius Urbicus** (*c.* AD 90 to after 139), the son of M. Lollius Senecio, a Berber Numidian landowner. An inscription (*CIL* VIII, 6706 = ILS 1065) found at Tiddis (a town in eastern Algeria) details each step of his career. After serving in two junior magistracies, he entered the army as a 'tribune with the broad stripe' (*tribunus laticlavius*) with *Legio* XXII *Primigenia* at Mogontiacum in Germania Superior. On completion he transferred to the staff of the proconsul of Asia as *quaestor*, whereafter he went to Rome and stood as a candidate for Tribune of the Plebs and later as one of the praetors. He returned to the army as legate of *Legio* X *Gemina* stationed in Pannonia, either at Aquincum or Vienna.

In far away Britannia, the governor at the time of the Jewish uprising was **Cn. Minicius Faustinus Sex. Iulius Severus** (*c.* AD 80 to after 136). He was born in the *colonia* Claudia Aequum (modern Čitluk near Sinj in Croatia) in the province of Dalmatia. An inscription from his home town (*CIL* III, 2830 = *ILS* 1056) preserves his illustrious career. After civilian and military postings (in Pannonia, AD 120–125), Hadrian picked Iulius Severus as his *legatus Augusti pro praetore* of Dacia (AD 126–127). He was elected suffect consul for the last quarter of AD 127. Thereafter he went as proconsul to Moesia Inferior (AD 128–132). In AD 132 Severus transferred to Britain where he had three legions, including VI *Victrix* and XX *Valeria Victrix*, and some 50 cohorts of auxiliaries under his command. Over his career he earned a reputation as one among the very best generals of his day. Cassius Dio describes him as 'a governor and leader who was just and prudent and a man of rank' (*Roman History* 69.14.4).

Other men of lower military rank who were active in theatre in Iudaea are known from inscriptions. Under the eagle standard of *Legio* X *Fretensis* were *tribunus* Aemilius Iuncus and *centurio* Octavius Secundus. With *Legio* III *Gallica* were *tribunus angusticlavius* M. Statius Priscus and centurion M. Sabidius Maximus. Sex. Attius Senecio was tribune of X *Gemina* when a detachment of his legion was dispatched from Pannonia to the war zone. Marching with *Legio* III *Cyrenaica* were *tribunus militum* C. Popilius Carus Pedo and reservist (or centurion) C. Nummius Constans.

One M. Censorius Cornelianus was *praepositus* in charge of a detachment of men from *Cohors* I *Hispanorum*. The title *praepositus* means 'overseer' or 'supervisor', indicating that he was an acting commander, not the officer of a regular unit. He dedicated an altar (*RIB* 3956) to Iupiter Augustus at Maryport, an outpost on the Cumbrian coast, located on the far western end of Hadrian's newly constructed wall. On the same inscription he is cited as *c[enturio] leg[ionis X Fr]etensis*, the legion stationed at the far eastern end of the Roman Empire. He may have accompanied Iulius Severus on his outbound journey from Britain. On reaching Iudaea he may have been re-assigned as a centurion with the legion and then, at the end of the war, returned to his former auxiliary cohort.

With less certainty, Q. Fuficius Cornutus saw action in the Bar Kokhba War. He was then a *tribunus laticlavius* of a legion now impossible to identify because of damage to the inscription (*AE* 1897, 19) found at Ager Histonii (modern Casalbordino). Another was Q. Albius Felix, who had been a *cornicularius* to a praetorian prefect earlier in his career. As a centurion – perhaps among the highest-ranking *primi ordines* – with *Legio* XX *Valeria Victrix* based at Deva (modern Chester) he was twice decorated, receiving *torques*, *armillae* and *phalerae* from the Emperor Trajan in person for valour in the Parthian War of AD 114–117. That achievement likely marked him out to take part in the war against the Jewish rebels.

All these men would be tested in battle and serve with distinction to re-establish Roman rule.

OPPOSING ARMIES

JEWISH FORCES

Shim'on ben Koseba's initial command centre was at Herodium, but his ultimate headquarters were located at the hilltop city of Betar. During the conflict he may have travelled widely throughout the war zone, to lead operations and motivate local units. From his base he communicated in handwritten memoranda with his deputies. Each town and village militia was called a camp (*mahaneh*). Significantly, the word is ideological and imbued with religious meaning. It is thus associated with holy warfare, which is consistent with the messianic vision of its supreme leader. A commander (*rosh hamahanaya*, literally 'head of the camp') was in charge of each *mahaneh*. This man was drawn from the local population and worked alongside the civilian *parnas*. From the surviving letters the administrative districts are known to have included Ein Gedi, Herodium, Ir-Nahash (Kirbet Natash near Herodium), Kiryat Arabaya and Tekoa. At the height of the rebellion, the area under insurgent control may have extended to border with Galilee and the Jewish Transjordan of Arabia Petraea. The leadership was not static; the extant letters indicate changes occurred during the war.

To seize and defend the Land of Israel, Ben Koseba needed an army (*tsaba*) of fit, motivated and committed men to serve in his ranks. He could appeal to the many discontented and distressed, or impoverished and indebted, all those struggling to make a living under the Roman occupation in Iudaea with the promise of a better life. Foremost among entry qualifications, he required all his soldiers to be Jewish. They would be fighting for their *moshiah*. Akiba had variously 12,000 'pair' (24,000) or even 48,000 students – according to Jewish sources, which likely inflate the actual number – attending his school of rabbinical studies at Beneberak, many of whom may have joined the war effort. As the rebellion gained momentum, men from outside the region – Galilee, the neighbouring Roman province of Arabia Petraea and Nabataea – would arrive to volunteer as fighters. It is evident that not all drawn to the fight for the freedom of Israel could communicate in the native languages (Aramaic and Hebrew) of the

The Jewish insurgents used several types of weapon. These iron three-bladed (trilobate) arrowheads from the Cave of Mount Yishai are likely captured Roman items. The tang attached the arrowhead to a shaft, either of wood or cane, which was then tied tightly with string. (Exhibit at the Israel Museum, Jerusalem. Author's collection)

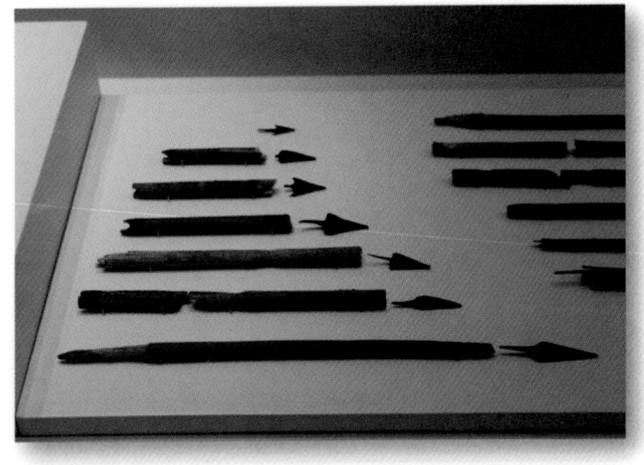

country, however. In one letter to Ben Koseba a Nabataean called Soumaios complains that he has to write in Greek because he cannot 'write in Hebrew letters' (*P. Yadin* 52).

Ben Koseba might have hoped to recruit from among the Christians, whose prophet had been born a Jew. But they decided that this was not their fight. They already had a messiah. The contemporary account of Justin (Iustinus Martyr), preserved by Eusebius, laments that the rebel leader required Christians 'to be punished severely if they did not deny Jesus as the Messiah and blaspheme him' (Eusebius, *Church History* 4.8.4). The other implication of this statement is that resident non-Jews could be forcibly conscripted into the rebel army.

The loyalty of Ben Koseba's soldiers, however, is never questioned in the literature. 'There were two brothers in Kefar Haruba,' the Midrash, *Lamentations* records, 'who did not allow any Romans to pass there'. Jewish religious texts preserve legendary stories of how Ben Koseba tested the courage and strength of his men. Those close to him at fortress Betar had amputated a finger to show their commitment to the cause. The sages were appalled at the self-inflicted mutilations and demanded to know, '"How long will you continue to make the men of Israel blemished?" He [Ben Koseba] asked them, "how else shall they be tested?" They answered, "let anyone who cannot uproot a cedar from Lebanon while riding a horse be refused enrollment in your army." So he had 200,000 of these and 200,000 of those' (Jerusalem Talmud).

The number of soldiers – 400,000 if the Talmud is to be believed – seems wildly exaggerated given the geographically small size of Iudaea. Perhaps the truer strength was a quarter or a third of that number, but that would still be an immense army. Cassius Dio puts the number of rebel casualties at the end of the conflict at '580,000 men' (*Roman History* 69.14.1). This claim also seems hyperbolical. All that can be inferred is that the army of the Jews under Ben Koseba's leadership numbered in the many tens of thousands of men.

Consistent with an insurgent guerrilla war strategy, the Jewish militiaman was typically lightly armed and ideally equipped for quick 'hit-and-run' attacks. Wearing a short tunic of homespun wool or linen, he may have fought with or without body armour according to his means. Examples of highly coloured fabrics – in up to 34 hues – have been found wonderfully preserved in the refuge caves at Ein Gedi. Tunics were simply two rectangular sheets of woven textiles stitched together at the shoulders with a slit for the head. The tunics often featured a contrasting stripe from the shoulder to knee on each of the left and right sides. For wear they could be tied at the waist with a belt or worn without one.

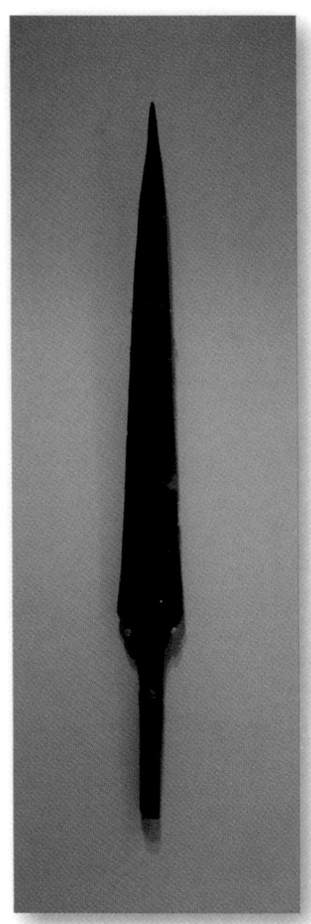

Jewish metalworkers are reported by Roman historian Cassius Dio to have secretly fashioned weapons before the rebel war began. This fine spearhead was found in the Cave of the Spear in the Judaean Hills. It may actually have been taken from the Roman army as a war spoil. (Exhibit at the Israel Museum, Jerusalem. Author's collection)

Sturdy footwear was essential in the terrain and heat of the Judaean countryside. These leather sandals feature soles of three layers of leather. Iron hobnails were commonly used to prolong the life of the soles. (Exhibit at the Israel Museum, Jerusalem. Author's collection)

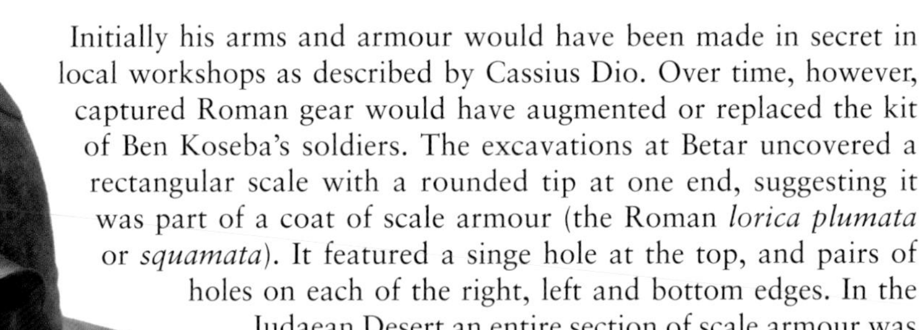

A helmet was a crucial item of the Roman soldier's kit. This complete and well-preserved specimen, dated to the 2nd century AD (the so-called 'Weisenau' or 'Imperial Italic G' type), is made of iron. The design, with integral neckguard, browguard and articulated cheekplates, features riveted cross bars to strengthen the dome from direct blows to the head. Unprovenanced, it is often mistakenly referred to as the 'Hebron Helmet'. (Exhibit at the Israel Museum, Jerusalem. Author's collection)

Initially his arms and armour would have been made in secret in local workshops as described by Cassius Dio. Over time, however, captured Roman gear would have augmented or replaced the kit of Ben Koseba's soldiers. The excavations at Betar uncovered a rectangular scale with a rounded tip at one end, suggesting it was part of a coat of scale armour (the Roman *lorica plumata* or *squamata*). It featured a singe hole at the top, and pairs of holes on each of the right, left and bottom edges. In the Judaean Desert an entire section of scale armour was found, composed of four rows, each made of six overlapping scales; a rebel coin was fused into one of the scales, dating it unequivocally to this period. Archaeologists working in the Cave of the Spear (in the Wadi Marrazah, north of Ein Gedi) found a single thin, rectangular copper plaque, measuring 2.5cm (1in.) by 1.5cm (½in.). Two holes were pierced in the upper corners. Another was found at the Teomin Cave on the lower slopes of the Judaean Mountains.

For defence he might carry a shield with a central boss and handgrip. A fragment of a wooden plank shield was discovered in a refuge cave. The shard of a single plank, measuring 8cm (3in.) by 3cm (1¼in.), has an acute-angled edge at the top indicating the complete shield was either hexagonal, oval or round in shape. A line of small holes along the top suggests the attachment of edging of stitched leather to protect the perimeter of the buckler. Useful in one-to-one combat, several men could assemble together in tight formation and form a defensive shield wall or phalanx in combination with swords or spears.

A rebel with a cause might just pick a stone from the ground and throw it. To increase his range and accuracy he could cast the stone with a sling. It was a simple weapon to make and use. Two lengths of twine were attached to a small cradle or pouch into which the projectile – a pebble, stone, or shot moulded of clay or lead – was placed. A slinger placed a finger through a loop on the end of one cord and the thumb and forefinger holding a tab at the end of the other cord. The sling was swung in an arc several times and the tab was released at a precise moment. The effectiveness of the weapon is highlighted in the Old Testament story of the duel in which David 'put his hand in his bag and took out a stone, slung it, and struck the Philistine on his forehead' and killed Goliath (1 *Samuel* 17:48–49). The great advantage of the sling was its simplicity (meaning it could be made at low cost from readily available materials) and its ease of use (meaning a soldier could reach proficiency after a few hours of training). A team occupying the high ground and equipped with slings and stones could launch a surprise attack on a marching column of Roman troops in the valley below and just as quickly disappear before the enemy could stage a counterattack.

A variety of edged weapons was available. The bow and arrow were used. Archery was widely practised in the region and often mentioned in rabbinic literature. A trained archer could fire arrows at a rapid rate and with precision over great distance. Simple flat, leaf-shaped arrowheads were found in the Caves of the Spear. Specimens of the trilobate – or three-winged – design were found in other locations. Twelve arrowheads have been found in the Har Yishai Caves on the extension of the Yishai Mountain at Ein Gedi, 11 of which were in perfect condition. They were of two designs; four of the blades were drawn back, while seven were 'cut' towards the sharpened end. Behind the blade was a narrow tang that was pushed into the wooden shaft. One was still attached to the shaft of the arrow and tightly wound with a strip of sinew to increase the bond. A near-complete arrow with its upper shaft and its three-winged blade in place was found near the entrance of the Cave of Letters at Nahal Hever. A further 30 specimens of the three-winged arrowhead have been found at Horvat 'Eqed, others at caves in the Nahal David and Nahal Arugot. These arrows were likely used with a composite bow. A grip made of bone (from an ibex endemic only to this region) was found at Herodium in a Bar Kokhba War context.

Roman military doctrine was to attack an enemy in massed formation on a battleground of their choosing. Having thrown missiles at medium-long range, the infantry advanced to engage in hand-to-hand combat, as depicted on this bas-relief from Glanum (Saint-Rémy-de-Provence) on display at the Fourvière Gallo-Roman Museum, France. (Rama, Wikimedia Commons, CC-BY-SA-2.0-fr)

Spears could be thrown as missiles at an enemy tens of metres away, or used to stab or slice an opponent at close quarters. Examples of bronze and iron blades were found in the Caves of the Spear (so named because several specimens were found there). They varied in length, breadth and profile. The specimens were generally flat leaf-shaped blades. One had a pyramid-shaped point and narrow shank typical of a Roman *pilum*. Indeed, it may have been a captured Roman weapon.

A sword or dagger could be fashioned by a Jewish metalworker or stripped from a fallen Roman soldier. As a last resort the war fighter might even use kitchen cutlery. A chopper and four knives with wooden and bone handles were found in a basket at the Cave of Letters at Nahal Hever. Easily concealed in the folds of a tunic, their iron blades could inflict deadly wounds. A curved knife called the *sica* was used by the bandits (after which they acquired the name *sicarii*) who made their last stand at Masada in AD 73.

A coat of chain mail (*lorica hamata*) was commonly worn by legionary and auxiliary troops serving in Hadrian's army. Made of thousands of small iron links riveted together, it weighed around 10kg (22lb). This fragment, the provenance of which is not recorded, was found packed in a helmet. (Exhibit at the Israel Museum, Jerusalem. Author's collection)

Well-made footwear was essential in the varied terrain of the conflict zone. Hobnails from the soles of open leather boots or military-style sandals have been found at many sites, including Herodium and several hideouts, including the Sabar Caves.

ROMAN FORCES

Hadrian's army (*exercitus*) was composed of professional soldiers. A freeborn Roman citizen could enrol in a legion at the age of 17 or 18. Having passed a health examination, he would receive a military mark and be sent to his unit. He signed on for 25 years and on completion of service was awarded a bonus. On arrival at camp he would receive basic training in drill, formations, riding, swimming and use of weapons, as well as route marching, camp building and siege warfare.

The new recruit would be assigned to a *centuria* of 80 men under the command of a centurion. Hadrian 'conferred the centurion's vine staff on those only who were hardy and of good repute' (Aelius Spartianus, *Life of Hadrian* 10.6). The centurion was assisted by a deputy (*optio*). Each century had a *signifer*, an officer who carried a military standard (*signum*) used to relay orders in concert with a horn player (*cornicen*). Six centuries formed a cohort (480 men), the first cohort being of double size. Ten cohorts formed a legion. A wing (*ala*) of 120 mounted soldiers provided an escort detail and courier service.

A legionary received a stipend in cash (paid three times a year). Deductions were made for food and equipment. His defensive gear included a helmet of bronze or iron with cheek plates, a brow guard and a neckguard. (A specimen dated to the 2nd century AD features iron cross-bands to strengthen the dome in case of a direct blow to the head.) Several types of body armour were in use in Hadrian's time: the shirt of chain mail (*lorica hamata*), made of individual iron links riveted together with shoulder doubling; the shirt of scale (*lorica plumata* or *squamata*), assembled from individual die-cut segments of bronze or iron and attached with wire or cord to a jerkin; and the articulated cuirass with shoulder protection (the so-called *lorica segmentata*), constructed from thin plates of iron riveted to leather bands on the inside. An apron (*cingulum*) of metal discs fixed to leather strips hung from a military belt. A curved shield – oval or rectangular in shape – made of a type of plywood, featured a central handgrip protected by an iron boss; a blazon painted on the exterior surface identified the legion.

After discharging the *pilum*, the Roman legionary engaged the enemy with shield and sword (*gladius*). The short, two-edged weapon was designed for stabbing and thrusting. A longer version (*spatha*) was used by cavalry. The corroded specimen shown here, from Mount Zion, Jerusalem, is still in its scabbard (*vagina*), complete with rings for attaching the baldric. (Exhibit at the Israel Museum, Jerusalem. Author's collection)

His weapons included the *pilum*, a 2m-long (6ft 7in.) javelin comprising a slender iron shaft with a pyramid-shaped tip attached to a wooden shank with a pin, which broke on impact so it could not be thrown back. In a massed formation, volleys of these *pila* could break an enemy line by piercing shields and pinning them together or wounding or killing the opponent. The bayonet-like *gladius* (sword) was some 60–65cm (24–26in.) long, with

Legionary cohorts often served away from their main home base camp on specific tactical missions. This inscription, carved into a slab of limestone in the 1st or 2nd century AD from Jerusalem or Samaria, reads: 'Legion X, Cohort IIX'; note the use of IIX rather than VIII for the number eight. (Exhibit at the Israel Museum, Jerusalem. Author's collection)

a double-edged blade 45–50cm (18–20in.) long. It was his close-quarters combat weapon for thrusting and stabbing. The short, leaf-shaped *pugio* (dagger) was a sidearm of last resort.

In command of a legion was a legate (*legatus legionis*), a senator personally appointed by Hadrian. Reporting to him in turn was a 'tribune of the broad stripe' (*tribunus angusticlavius*), a young man marked out for promotion – again by Hadrian – through the Roman political, legal and military career ladder. He was assisted by a team of five 'tribunes of the narrow stripe' (*tribuni laticlavii*), generally teenagers just starting out on their careers. Hadrian 'appointed as tribunes only men with full beards or of an age to give to the authority of the tribuneship the full measure of prudence and maturity' (Aelius Spartianus, *Life of Hadrian* 10.6). Ranked third in the chain of command was a camp prefect (*praefectus castrorum*). He was

Ti. Claudius Fatalis was a native of the city of Rome, who enrolled in the army when 19 years old. He served with several legions in Britain and Germany before arriving in Jerusalem where his rank was centurion *tertius hastatus* in *Legio* X *Fretensis*. He died aged 42. He freed from slavery the woman he married, who erected the stele, which is dated AD 70–175. (Exhibit at the Israel Museum, Jerusalem. Author's collection)

In peacetime, legionaries could be called upon to perform civil engineering duties. This inscription, dating to around AD 130, reads: '*Imperator* Caesar Traianus Hadrianus made [the aqueduct] by [means of] a vexillation of *Legio* X *Fretensis*'. Other inscriptions also record *Legiones* II and VI as having made repairs to the same aqueduct near Caesarea. (Exhibit at the Israel Museum, Jerusalem. Author's collection)

responsible for administration, training, logistics, managing the legion on the march, establishing the camp, maintenance of artillery and conducting siege warfare. Next in the hierarchy was the chief centurion (*centurio primus pilus*). The legion at full strength could number some 5,600 men-at-arms.

There were 30 legions in service in AD 132. The theoretical strength of Hadrian's army was thus some 168,000 men. His order of battle was arranged into army groups by province. The consular provinces were administered by governors appointed by the Senate, the other territories (called praetorian) by Hadrian. His own legal powers permitted him to pick a deputy to govern each province. Every *legatus Augusti pro praetore* was responsible for ensuring the security of his province and, to do so, he commanded all the military units stationed there.

In addition to legions, there were units of professional non-Roman citizen soldiers. These auxiliary units were drafted from conquered peoples and allies. After completing a term of service with honour the auxiliaryman could look forward to being awarded citizenship, confirmed in an official document (the so-called diploma). There were three kinds of tactical unit: the *ala* of 480 or 720 cavalry; the *cohors peditata* of 480 or 800 men; and the *cohors equitata* of mixed cavalry/infantry of 600 or 1,040 men. They were commanded by a *praefectus* (or a *tribunus militum* in certain units). In total the *auxilia* provided approximately 218,000 men for the Roman army at this time. Their equipment was similar to that of the legionaries: helmet, body armour (chain mail rather than plate), *gladius* for the infantry or longer *spatha* for the cavalry and a spear (*lancea*, about 2m (6ft 7in.) in length).

Available to support the land-based forces were fleets of the Roman navy. These patrolled the seas and rivers keeping piracy and banditry in check, and assisted with moving men and *matériel* in war time. A warship could be powered by a rigged mainsail and artemon, or oars (the rowers being arranged in two-banks in a *liburna* or three in a trireme). A *liburna* might be 27m (90ft) long and was steered by a pair of side rudders mounted aft, operated from a poop-deck. The ship was fitted with a built-up forecastle and a bronze beaked prow (*rostrum*) at sea level. The crew of a *liburna* comprised 62 oarsmen and six sailors, captained by a *trierarchos*. The ship's combat unit of 15 marines (all auxiliaries) was commanded by a centurion, who also had an *optio* and specialists to assist him. Ten such vessels may have formed a squadron commanded by a *navarchus* who reported to an equestrian *praefectus classis*.

In AD 132 in Iudaea there were two legions (11,200 men-at-arms at full strength):

Legio VI *Ferrata* – at Tel Shalem in the Beth Shean Valley, it moved into Iudaea sometime after AD 120 to replace *Legio* II *Traiana Firma*. Previously the legion had been part of Trajan's expeditionary army in the Parthian War, after which it transferred to Arabia Petraea.

Legio X *Fretensis* – encamped in the ruined city of Hierosolyma, it had a long association in the province. Many men of the legion were likely seconded away in Caesarea with the *praefectus* providing staff for his administrative office, and carrying out repairs to the public infrastructure, such as the aqueduct supplying the city with fresh water.

Additionally, there were up to six units of auxiliaries (9,500 soldiers) in Iudaea including:

Cohors I *Miliaria Thracum* – at Beit Guvrin (the precursor to the later city of Eleutheropolis), its presence is confirmed by the find of a tile. The cohort was transferred in from Syria and was active in Iudaea from AD 124. Its main base camp at Beit Guvrin was a square enclosure covering 3 hectares (7½ acres), a space large enough for a 1,000-strong auxiliary cohort. A detachment was stationed at Ein Gedi.

Ala Antiana Gallorum et Thracum Sagittaria – also at Beit Guvrin, a unit of cavalry (which fought with bows) is attested by floor tiles stamped with the unit's moniker at the site.

In times of emergency a *legatus Augusti* could request assistance from the commander-in-chief. Governors in neighbouring provinces could release entire legions, which marched under their own eagles (*aquilae*), or individual or multiple cohorts marching under detachment flags (*vexilla*). Pioneered by Augustus and Tiberius, these vexillations could combine with units from other legions to form a tactical field army to address the particular crisis at hand. In these forms contingents of troops drawn from all over the empire served in the Bar Kokhba War.

From Syria:

Legio III *Gallica* – stationed at Raphanaea (al-Rafniye, halfway between Antioch and Damascus), it may have taken part in Trajan's wars in Dacia and Parthia. A vexillation of III *Gallica* was already in Iudaea in AD 116.

Classis Syriacae – the home port of Syria's navy was Seleucia Pieria from where it patrolled the eastern Mediterranean. A squadron may have been deployed to police the Dead Sea and monitor marine activity.

Auxilia – three *alae* and 12 *cohortes* are attested in Syria in a diploma dated to AD 139.

From Arabia Petraea:

Legio III *Cyrenaica* – stationed at Bostra (Busra al-Sham), it was one of the legions that fought in the Jewish War and was at the siege of Hierosolyma in AD 70. The legion was transferred to Arabia Petraea after its annexation in AD 106. It then moved to Egypt, where it was likely involved in suppressing the uprising of Jews in Alexandria, and may have seen action in the Parthian War. By AD 125 it was back in Arabia Petraea.

From Cappadoceia:

Legio XII *Fulminata* – encamped at Melitene, the legion had been part of Trajan's expeditionary force to Parthia. When Hadrian abandoned Babylonia and Mesopotamia in AD 117–118 it returned to Cappadoceia.

From Egypt:

Legio II *Traiana Fortis* – based at Alexandria, the legion was founded by Trajan in AD 105 to fight in his Dacian War. After the conflict it may have gone to Arabia Petraea (where it would have joined III *Cyrenaica*) or moved to a base on the Danube. In preparation for Trajan's Parthian War, it moved to Syria. Thereafter it (or part of it) went to Iudaea, where the presence of troops at Caesarea is revealed by an inscription on an aqueduct.

Legio XXII *Deiotoriana* – sharing its camp at Alexandria with *Legio* II *Traiana Fortis* it is recorded on a document listing legions dated to AD 119 (or 123).

From Pannonia Superior:

Legio X *Gemina* – encamped at Vindobona (Vienna). It may have been involved in Trajan's Second Dacian War, but its main mission appears to have been to patrol the Danube River.

From Moesia Inferior:

Legio V *Macedonica* – based at Troesmis (Iglita), part of it was dispatched to fight in Trajan's Parthian War or to Syria. Its presence during the Bar Kokhba War is attested by an inscription.

Legio XI *Claudia* – stationed at Durostorum (Silistra) in Moesia Inferior, it likely took part in Trajan's Dacian War. One of its responsibilities was to protect the Greek-speaking communities of the Crimea. An inscription confirms it took part in the Bar Kokhba War.

Legio XIV *Gemina* – located at Carnuntum (Petronell), an epitaph from Gadara suggests cohorts from the legion were in action during the Bar Kokhba War, but it is disputed.

From Britannia:

Legio VI *Victrix* – though based at Eboracum (York) its presence in Iudaea is suggested by an interpretative reading of a floor tile stamp found at Beit Guvrin.

Legio XX *Valeria Victrix* – stationed at Deva (Chester), the legion had been in Britain since AD 43. It had played a part in crushing the rebellion of Boudica and the Iceni (AD 60–61). Men of *Legio* XX had helped in the building of Hadrian's Wall (AD 122–128).

Cohors I *Hispanorum milliaria* – encamped at Maryport, Cumbria, the unit was an 800-man infantry cohort.

Cohors IV *Lingonum* – based at Wallsend, Tyne and Wear, the unit was a 600-man infantry cohort.

The actual number of troops Hadrian sent to crush the insurgency is difficult to calculate with any accuracy. *Legiones* VI *Ferrata*, X *Fretensis* and III *Gallica*, plus the local *auxilia*, took part as complete units. Many other legions and auxiliaries supplemented them as vexillations. The combined force deployed in theatre at the height of the war could, thus, have numbered as few as 25,000 or as many as 45,000. Given that the total force available at the time was some 443,000, either number represented a sizeable investment of men and *matériel* in regional conflict.

Auxiliary units (*alae*) provided the majority of cavalry troops in the Roman army. Their primary function was to support infantry on the battlefield, but they could be deployed on patrols and exploratory missions. This stele in the Römisch-Germanisches Museum, Cologne shows the defensive equipment a rider used included a helmet, chain-mail coat and an oval shield (*scutum*), the weaponry a spear (*lancea*) and a long sword (*spatha*). (Wikimedia Commons, CC-BY-SA-3.0-de)

OPPOSING PLANS

JEWISH PLANS

Ben Koseba's primary objectives were to free the ancient Land of Israel from Roman occupation and to liberate the city of Jerusalem. His was a messianic vision of redemption with himself as warrior in chief. The extent to which this meant establishing an independent self-governing Jewish state is still debated. It was a venture of the highest risk; the price of failure would be very great indeed. To succeed, he would need to understand the strengths and weaknesses of his enemy, and to prepare both for a protracted war and his people's survival. The lessons of past insurrections (of the First Jewish War six decades before and of AD 115–117) would surely have informed his strategy formulation and tactical planning.

Firstly, he had to determine where to launch his revolt. Permanent Roman garrisons were concentrated in the north of the province of Iudaea in the district of Galilee and in Jerusalem. Taking the entire province would be futile until he could raise sufficient forces to match or exceed those of the occupying army. For historical and religious reasons the civilian population in Samaria was unlikely to throw its support behind the Jewish cause. An

The fertile land of the Judaean Shephelah produced a variety of crops that could sustain the population of the independent Jewish state led by Shim'on ben Koseba. Called the 'land flowing with milk and honey' (*Deuteronomy* 31:20), the Midrash explains that milk symbolizes superior quality, richness of taste and nourishment, while honey represents sweetness. Israel is thus both nourishing and pleasant. (Author's collection)

attainable goal would be to seize the district of Iudaea, bordered in the north by Samaria, by Idumaea in the south, the Mediterranean in the west and the Dead Sea in the east. The terrain – and the Judaean Desert and Shephelah in particular – would also work to the advantage of the revolutionaries. If Ben Koseba could demonstrate that his rebellion had legs, disenchanted Jews and other sympathizers elsewhere might join his followers in Iudaea or escalate the troubles consuming the Romans by fomenting uprisings in their own regions, such as in Galilee or Arabia Petraea. This way the rebellion might spread well beyond its epicentre. In the name of peace, perhaps then the head of the Roman world might be willing to reach an accommodation with the leader of the Jewish nation.

This lead weight from the Horvat Alim (Beit Guvrin area) bears the paleo-Hebrew inscription 'Shim'on ben Koseba, Prince of Israel' and the name of his *parnas* Shim'on Dasoi. *Parnasim* enforced rules and regulations for commerce and trade in the rebel-held administrative districts. It weighs 803.6 grammes (1lb 12oz). (Exhibit at the Israel Museum, Jerusalem. Author's collection)

Seizing Iudaea would mean ousting the Roman garrisons in the region. In Ben Koseba's favour, the Roman military presence was lighter in Iudaea than in either Galilee or Samaria. The relatively small numbers of Roman troops scattered along the roads and among the towns could be overwhelmed by organized bands of armed fighters – just as bandits had done for decades. He would find eager soldiers among the disaffected and the poor, as well as idealistic young Jewish men (like the two brothers in Kefar Haruba mentioned above) who shared his dream and burned with a desire to liberate Israel from the Roman foe. They would have heard the war stories and tales of heroism by Jews like them in Cyprus, Libya and Egypt, and how they had resisted the Roman invasion of Mesopotamia. Outraged by reports of the Roman emperor's plans to strike at the very heart of their faith and identity, these patriots would be motivated to fight to take their people's destiny into their own hands.

An oasis supported a community on the western shore of the Dead Sea. Its prosperity derived from processing balsam, an ingredient used in perfumes. A harbour (yet to be identified by archaeologists) allowed ships to berth after crossing from Arabia Petraea on the far shore. (Author's collection)

Twelve kilometres south of Jerusalem stands Herod the Great's fortified palace. A bird's-eye view of the Herodium reveals the geometric defensive architecture of the fortress built on the crest of the mound. Beneath it, rebels loyal to Shim'on ben Koseba dug extensive tunnels. (Hebrew Wikipedia Project)

Ben Koseba's rebel army would need to covertly amass an extensive armoury of weapons to withstand a war with well-equipped Roman troops. In one Roman source it is claimed that Jewish metalworkers commissioned to provide the Roman army with equipment 'purposely made of poor quality such weapons as they were called upon to furnish, in order that the Romans might reject them and they themselves might thus have the use of them' (Cassius Dio, *Roman History* 69.12.2). The historian's statement might contain a kernel of truth. The subject peoples of the Romans were often required to pay taxes in cash or kind, some of which (such as foodstuffs, animal hides or clothing) would be supplied to the army. The Jews certainly had the skills and the means. A foundry has been identified at Herodium that is contemporary with the war. Smithy tools have been found at Betar, including iron anvils, hammerheads, tongs and chisels. With them an armourer could both produce new equipment, and adapt and repair damaged pieces.

Secondly, having taken territory, Ben Koseba would need a plan to govern, sustain and defend it. The spiritual home of Judaism was Hierosolyma. Liberating it would be an important medium- or long-term aim of the rebel leader, one that would drive his ambition and inspire his soldiers. But the city was still occupied by crack Roman troops of *Legio* X. Until it could be taken, he needed a base from which to direct operations. As his command centre he may have initially chosen Herodium. Situated 15km (9 miles) south-southeast of the ruined city, it was a near impregnable – and now abandoned – fortress built by Herod the Great (74/73–5/4 BC) and the old king was buried there. However, Betar, a hilltop city 10km (6 miles) south-west of Hierosolyma on the road to Gaza, would become the final headquarters of the national resistance.

As *Nasi' Yisra'el* he would quickly need to set up institutions to govern the new nation and convince those living in the communities within its nominal boundary that it was legitimate and worth supporting. He would need the support of the upper and middle economic classes to make it function. The goal would be 'business as usual', except that everywhere the rebels held territory Jewish civil and criminal law (as interpreted by the rabbis) would replace Roman. To minimize disruption, however, the administrative districts would be based on existing Roman jurisdictions. From the surviving letters these are known to have included Betar, Ein Gedi, Herodium, Ir-Nahash (Kirbet Natash near Herodium), Kiryat Arabaya and Tekoa. The territory may have extended across the Jordan River. Each community would be managed jointly by a civilian administrator (*parnas*) and a militia commander reporting direct to Ben Koseba. The *parnasim* authorized land leases, oversaw weights and measures and minted coins. They collected the annual rent from tenants leasing land belonging to the head of state, ten per cent of which was apparently paid into the national treasury to support the revolutionary state.

The upstart nation would need to feed its population and nurture its fledgling economy. Access to the markets in the Roman Empire would effectively be closed off by war (unless goods were smuggled in and out). The people of Ben Koseba would, instead, need to develop self-sufficiency and look East. The people of Iudaea were resourceful farmers (producing fruit, honey, meat, olive oil, vegetables, wheat and wine in abundance) and talented traders (in leather and metal goods). On the edge of the arid Judaean Desert lay Ein Gedi, a natural spring. It was the most important oasis on the western shore of the Dead Sea. The small town, located between Nahal David and Nahal Arugot, prospered on the back of trade in balsam. Used in perfumes, it was extracted from the persimmon plant and its processing as a resin was a guarded trade secret because of its high resale value. The town produced other cash crops too, like salt, asphalt and dates. Palm branches and citrons (*citrus medica*) grown here also played an important role in religious ritual. Sheep rearers brought their flocks down from the Judaean Hills during the winter months. Caravans also stopped to trade at the market in Ein Gedi and enjoy its cool, fresh water and to take a bath. With a harbour (*mahoz*), the town's location on the Dead Sea and access to Arabia Petraea and the lands beyond to the east may have made it strategically valuable in Ben Koseba's plan for the Land of Israel's independence.

Lastly, defending his new nation from the certain retaliation of the Roman authorities was Ben Koseba's harder to achieve military objective. He clearly believed he could achieve it. History showed that it *could* be done. During the years 147–139 BC Viriathus had successfully led his people – the Lusitani – to freedom, even reaching a settlement with a Roman consul (until he was assassinated by men from his own side, bribed by other Romans intent on outright conquest). In AD 9 Arminius had led a coalition of Germanic nations that permanently ousted the army of Caesar Augustus from land on the right bank of the Rhine. Like them, Ben Koseba would need to exploit his opponent's weaknesses while reducing to a minimum his own. Crucial to the long-term success of his insurgency in Iudaea would be to avoid (at all costs) set-piece battles against professional troops.

His would be a campaign of asymmetric warfare. Unpredictability would be his winning strategy. It would be a war of attrition. Ambushes would wear down the heavily armed, but slow-moving columns of Roman soldiers marching through Iudaea. The Jews would use their knowledge of local terrain to pick the best and most advantageous positions from which to launch hit-and-run attack missions. To avoid detection and discovery, they would conceal their warriors and weapons underground in caves. Hewn

The Jewish rebels expanded the tunnel network in the Herodium mound dug by their antecedents in the First Jewish War (AD 66–70). The new tunnels were deeper and wider than the earlier structures to allow more troops to assemble and disgorge from the exits hidden from the casual observer outside. (Carole Raddato, CC BY-SA 2.0)

out of the living rock, these offered 'places of refuge whenever they should be hard pressed, and might meet together unobserved under ground; and they pierced these subterranean passages from above at intervals to let in air and light' (Cassius Dio, *Roman History* 69.12.3).

Some 140 caves and hiding places have been found in Israel and the West Bank. Fighting underground was fraught with danger. It relied on surprise – the Romans not knowing where the Jews would strike. Herodium, for example, was a conspicuous target: it is the highest peak in the Judaean Desert, rising to 758m (2,487ft) above sea level. The element of surprise required a creative approach. Ben Koseba's men entered the cisterns beneath the fortified palace originally constructed by Herod's engineers and excavated tunnels deep into the mound. The rebels dug them to be broad and high to facilitate movement of large numbers of soldiers. These tunnels traced through the mound ending in sally ports (two of which were beside the tomb of the great king). Normally they would be covered to hide them. When the Romans scaled Herodium, its defenders would quietly assemble in the tunnels, suddenly emerge through the openings and attack the enemy en masse from behind.

In the lowlands too, rebel soldiers could emerge covertly and launch ambushes on unsuspecting Roman troops. The underground complexes in the Judaean Shephelah (such as Horvat 'Amuda, Horvat Naqiq and Khirbet Binaya), however, seem to be designed with *defence* as the primary criterion. Often adapting earlier hiding places, the Jews fiendishly designed their tunnels to be narrow (reducing access to just a single man), and to meander (often curving in a direction which exposed the intruder's side unprotected by a shield). Labyrinthine connections could quickly disorient anyone entering and unfamiliar with the layout. In the darkness, an infiltrator would not be able to see unless by lamplight, and the very illumination betrayed his position to the defender who was enshrouded in darkness. Tunnels ended in nodes or chambers where the intruder could be ambushed. Carved of rock there was nothing to burn, and any combustible material brought in and set alight by the interlopers might create smoke that simply blew back in their faces, drawn by the backdraft from openings cut into the ceilings.

Above ground across the region, the rebels fortified their homesteads, farms and villages with stout defensive walls and high observation towers. One such is Horvat Zalit. It is situated approximately 1.5km (1 mile) south-east of Meitar on a spur overlooking Nahal Eshtemo'a on the southern slopes of the Judaean Shephelah. It was a fortified building consisting of a square tower and a courtyard surrounded by rooms. Within the courtyard was an extensive water system connected to pools of water (*mikwa'ot*) for ritual bathing. The Romans would need to capture this location – and every other one like it – to crush the rebellion. The process of doing so would delay their advance, buying the rebels time to regroup and stage counterattacks.

All of this would take careful planning over months (if not years) and the collusion of a great many people who must be trusted to keep the plot secret from the Romans.

ROMAN PLANS

As the military governor, Tineius Rufus' priority was to keep his province *pacata atque quieta*, 'pacified and quiet' (Ulpian, *Digest* 1.18.13.pr.). The legalistically minded Romans regarded rebellion (*seditio*) as a breach of treaty – an injury (*iniuria*) to the Roman people – which must be met with revenge (*ultio*). The traditional response was *vastatio*, a devastating punitive war intended to send the unequivocal message that resistance would not be tolerated. When the Jews rose in AD 66 they had been met with force. During that war the Romans demonstrated an astonishing determination to reduce those who challenged their authority, however long it took. Eight years were needed finally to break the insurgents' resolve, but in the end victory went to Rome. Capital punishment faced those captured and charged with sedition. After the Judaean Revolt of 4 BC (which was provoked by the mismanagement of *Procurator* Sabinus) the *Legatus Augusti* of Syria, P. Quinctilius Varus, showed clemency and forgave the mass of those who had rebelled; but he singled out for harsh punishment the relations of Herod who had taken part and crucified 2,000 of their followers.

Learning of a violent outbreak, uppermost in the senior commander's mind would be to determine the location and extent of the challenge to his authority. The situation would be dynamic, but in forming his assessment he would be assisted by a constant flow of military intelligence. Deployed across Iudaea were specialist soldiers (*stationarii*) who acted as highway police, manned tollhouses and patrolled for bandit activity. The centurions, tribunes or prefects of units on the ground encountering any trouble were empowered to respond with force. They would relay messages up the line in the chain of command. The newly expanded road network would assist in expediting transmission of these communications. The region had a history of banditry and short-lived campaigns of subversion, often inspired by cult leaders. These minor infractions could be dealt with relatively quickly and with an economy of force. However, if the local unit needed assistance, provincial command in *colonia* Caesarea would be advised. Once received, the staff of

The open plains of the Judaean Shephelah favoured the combat doctrine of the Roman army. With his lightly armed troops Shim'on ben Koseba would need to use the terrain of Iudaea to level the odds and defeat the enemy intent on crushing him. Underground caves were his secret assets. (Author's collection)

the office would advise the *legatus Augusti*, who would authorize sending reinforcements as he deemed necessary to address the threat. It would take time, however, to mobilize large numbers of troops and *matériel* from the legate's army group.

Roman military strategy was predicated on bringing the enemy to fight in the open in a set-piece battle, or containing him in a siege. The calculus did not necessarily require overwhelming force. Romans believed that training, discipline and technology generally won against an indisciplined rabble, even when the odds were seemingly weighted against them. Preparation was key to success, and statistical information about resources was the basis for sound strategic and tactical planning.

The process of collating such information was labour intensive. Each centurion kept a daily roster (written by hand in ink on wooden sheets or papyrus) that recorded where his individual soldiers were assigned and what duties they were performing – even if they were sick or serving time in prison. Morning reports collated this granular detail into summaries by unit name, showing numbers of personnel (soldiers and officers) fit for duty, departures and so on. Every year clerks prepared (normally on 31 December) a high-level summary report (*pridianum*) of the unit's location, date of arrival there, net numerical strength, as well as numbers of promotions and transfers in, transfers out, losses, new recruits, discharges and other germane information. Though already several months out of date, Tineius Rufus would, nevertheless, have been able quickly to access the resources available to him in the summer of AD 132.

The decisions Rufus made in the early weeks of learning about the Jewish insurgency would determine the course and length of the coming war.

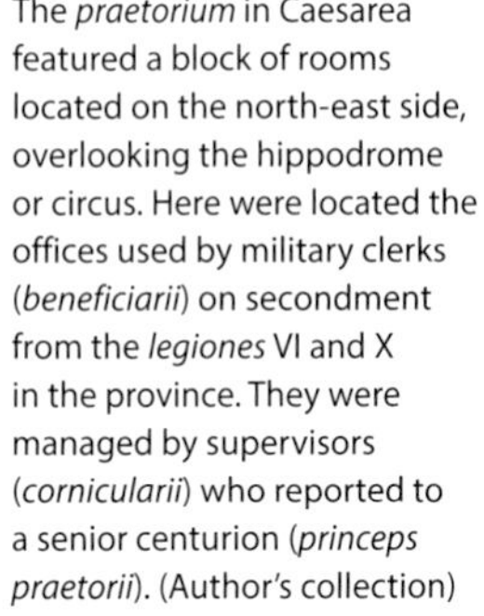

The *praetorium* in Caesarea featured a block of rooms located on the north-east side, overlooking the hippodrome or circus. Here were located the offices used by military clerks (*beneficiarii*) on secondment from the *legiones* VI and X in the province. They were managed by supervisors (*cornicularii*) who reported to a senior centurion (*princeps praetorii*). (Author's collection)

THE CAMPAIGN

'FOR THE FREEDOM OF JERUSALEM'

'So long as Hadrian was close by in Egypt and again in Syria, they remained quiet,' writes Cassius Dio (*Roman History* 69.12.2). Over the two years since the Roman commander-in-chief had departed the province, Ben Koseba had risen to become leader of an armed resistance movement. He used the time to spread his message of redemption and to rally support from Jewish communities throughout Iudaea.

He received a major boost to his status when he was declared the *moshiah*. It is claimed that Rabbi Akiba interpreted the messianic prophecy in *Numbers* 24:17 – 'there shall come a star (*kohav*) out of Ya'akob – and coined the moniker 'Bar Kokhba' ('son of a star') for Shim'on ben Koseba. There were, however, dissenters: 'When Rabbi Akiba beheld Bar Koseba he exclaimed: "This is the King Messiah!" Rabbi Yohanan ben Torta retorted: "Akiba, grass will grow in your cheeks and still the son of David will not have come"' (Jerusalem Talmud, *Ta'anit* 4:5).

The endorsement of the highly influential rabbi of Beneberak was crucial in validating him as the military leader of the Jews in their war of liberation. Based on his commendation, thousands – including many of his own students – flocked to the man they now called the Bar Kokhba. Rabbi Shim'on bar

Roman troops marched by cohort in lines, carrying some 25kg (55lb) of arms, equipment and personal effects, as depicted on Trajan's Column. The legionary was expected to march 20 Roman miles in five hours on a day in summer at normal 'military step' (*militaris gradus*), but in wartime a forced march (*magna itinera*) at the swifter 'full step' (*plenus gradus*) could increase this to 24 miles. (Public Domain)

Judaea Campaign, AD 132–133

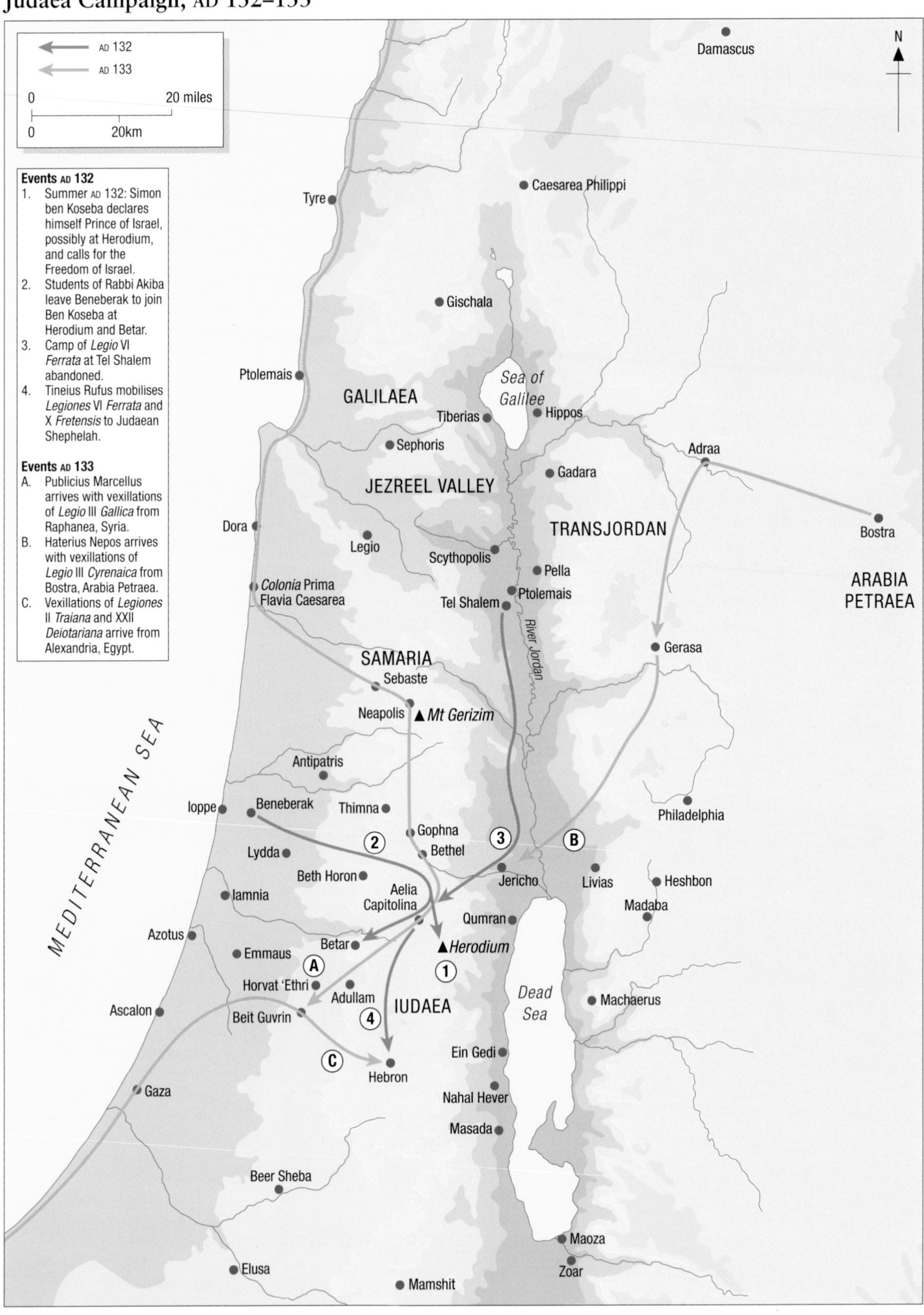

Yochai was one of them. Out of view of the Romans, they began carefully excavating hiding places and underground tunnels, fortifying villages and amassing arms and armour in readiness for the coming violent clash.

The exact date that marked the start of the war, which would have the greatest consequences for the Jews of Iudaea, is lost to time. The first year of the conflict is confirmed as AD 132 by Eusebius in his *Chronicle* under the entry for 'Hadrian's Year 16'. Summer is the most likely season – after the Hebrew month of *Iyyar*, perhaps in *Tishri*. The event which launched the rebellion is also unrecorded. Perhaps on a pre-agreed day, the rebels began attacking Roman military patrols wherever they encountered them. Along the roads of Iudaea, Jewish forces ambushed the unsuspecting troops moving through the country. They took advantage of the Romans' vulnerabilities. On the march they were laden with their personal effects hanging from poles over their shoulders. Their heads were often unprotected because they tied their helmets to their body armour. Their shields were usually wrapped in protective leather covers, which added weight. Mules and waggons slowed the army on the march. Roman troops could not react quickly when faced with hit-and-run attacks. Showers of arrows, sling stones and spears thrown at distance caused casualties among the ordered but densely packed Roman lines of troops marching four or more abreast. In towns and villages Jews turned on the Roman soldiers deployed on policing duties, assaulting them from behind and cutting their throats, or stoning them and firing arrows at them from above.

The initial Roman response was almost dismissive. 'At first,' writes Dio, 'the Romans took no account of them' (Cassius Dio, *Roman History* 69.13.1). Iudaea was known for sporadic acts of violence. Tineius Rufus could reasonably expect that his local unit commanders would deal with the infractions as they arose. The troublemakers would eventually be overcome by superior discipline, training, equipment and tactics of the soldiers of *Legiones* VI *Ferrata* based in Galilee and X *Fretensis* in Jerusalem. However, trained in the combat doctrine of the bandit, Ben Koseba was fighting an

Apparently out of nowhere, Jewish insurgents would appear and inflict heavy casualties on the unsuspecting Roman troops. Rebel soldiers gathered in caves and launched hit-and-run attacks, causing heavy casualties. (Author's collection)

REBELS PLOTTING THEIR NEXT MISSION IN A HIDING CAVE (PP. 42–43)

To establish and hold the Jewish state of Israel, Shim'on ben Koseba relied on a strategy of waging a war of attrition against the occupying Romans. 'They occupied the advantageous positions in the country and strengthened them with mines and walls,' writes Cassius Dio (*Roman History* 56.12.3). Across the Judaean Shephelah local people exploited the quality of the geology beneath their feet to excavate networks of tunnels, nodes and chambers.

In this reconstruction scene Jewish rebels loyal to Ben Koseba meet in the underground hiding complex at the village at Horvat Naqiq near Tel Bet Mirsham. The commander **(1)** of the local camp (*mahaneh*) explains a mission he has planned to a group of heads of households **(2)** from other farms and villages located in his jurisdiction. These men pay ten per cent of their earnings annually into the national treasury to support the revolutionary state. The commander is in direct communication with Shim'on ben Koseba at his headquarters. The self-styled *Nasi' Yisra'el* ('Prince Over Israel') regularly writes to his militia leaders. Tough, uncompromising and sometimes harsh, he demands complete obedience from them and urges them to take action to keep their young nation secure.

From these and similar underground caves the Jews have successfully launched many hit-and-run ambushes upon columns of Roman legionaries marching through their lands. Intimately knowledgable about the local terrain, the local militias know the best places to lie in wait. They have trained in the skills of the bandit and skirmisher. A weapon can be as simple as a stone, picked up off the ground and shaped into an aerodynamic bullet. Thrown with a sling, the slingshot's impact can be deadly. In the years before the outbreak of the revolt, Jewish metalworkers also fabricated arrows, spears and swords for such local militias, arsenals of which have since been built up by gathering captured Roman weapons **(3)** after waging successful attacks.

In some of the local fortified farmsteads, seized Roman coins are being overstruck with new images and messages approved by Ben Koseba's regime. 'For the Freedom of Jerusalem' is a recurring theme of the rebellion. Fulfilling the dream motivates Jews loyal to the national military leader they regard as the 'King Messiah' – a view validated by Rabbi Akiba ben Yosef who, interpreting the prophecy in *Numbers* 24:17, calls *Bar Kokhba* ('son of a star').

aggressive guerrilla war. He knew the strengths and weaknesses of his forces – and those of his opponent. 'To be sure,' writes Cassius Dio, 'they did not dare try conclusions with the Romans in the open field' (*Roman History* 69.12.3). Instead, 'they occupied the advantageous positions in the country and strengthened them with mines and walls, in order that they might have places of refuge whenever they should be hard pressed' (Cassius Dio, *Roman History* 69.12.3).

'They occupied the advantageous positions in the country,' writes Cassius Dio (*Roman History*, 69.12.3). From high vantage points the insurgents could track the movement of Roman troops and launch ambuscades – firing arrows and slingshot upon their lines – with deadly effect. Even today visitors have to beware of openings to ancient underground hideouts hidden by undergrowth. (Author's collection)

The insurgent leader's operational strategy worked remarkably well and the region was soon 'devastated' (Eusebius, *Chronicle*). Buoyed by their early successes, Ben Koseba's *parnasim* began to mint coins. They took Roman silver and bronze coins and overstruck them with images of their own choosing. The high denomination *tetradrachma* became the *shekel* (or Neronian *sel'a*), the *denarius* and provincial *drachma* was repurposed as the *zuz*, while the *sestertius*, *dupondius* and *as* became *prutah*, or small change. As they hammered the dies, they obliterated the symbols of Roman pagan worship and replaced them with new ones emphasizing the religious objectives of the revolutionary war. One issue of the repurposed coins now carried the message 'Year One of the Redemption of Israel' with an image of a vine leaf on one side, and the name 'Shim'on' with a palm tree with seven branches and two clusters of dates on the other side. Another design displayed a bunch of grapes in high relief with the legend 'Year One of the Redemption of Jerusalem' on one surface and, on the other, a palm tree with two bunches of dates and the name 'Eleazer the Priest' (Ben Koseba's presumed second in command).

Encouraged by the success of the rebellion, Jews still living in Roman-controlled territory fled to the relative sanctuary of the land under the protection of the 'Prince of Israel'. In neighbouring Arabia Petraea a Jewish woman left her comfortable residence in Mehoza (modern Maoza, Jordan) and set off for Ein Gedi, which was now under rebel control. Named Babatha she came from a wealthy family and had married a man called Judah who owned three date orchards near the oasis town on the Dead Sea. According to documents, which survive, in AD 128 he had taken an interest-free loan from his wife. He died two years later and Babatha took the orchards in settlement of the outstanding loan. However,

In this cuirassed statue, Hadrian is shown as military commander (*imperator*). It was discovered in 1975 at the site of the base of *Legio* VI *Ferrata* at Tel Shalem in the Beth Shean Valley. The level of workmanship in bronze suggests it was cast in Italy. The statue had, apparently, been purposely buried in the ground. (Exhibit at the Israel Museum, Jerusalem. Author's collection)

Judah's first wife, Miriam, who was herself at Ein Gedi, brought an action against Babatha over her late husband's property at the local court. Even as war raged in the Judaean Hills and Shephelah, the two litigants evidently felt sufficiently confident in the rebel administration under its *parnas* approved by Ben Koseba to conduct their legal business in the town.

Rufus had seriously underestimated his adversary: 'Soon, however, all Iudaea had been stirred up, and the Jews everywhere were showing signs of disturbance, were gathering together, and giving evidence of great hostility to the Romans, partly by secret and partly by overt acts' (Cassius Dio, *Roman History* 69.13.1).

In their camp at Tel Shalem, the legionaries of VI *Ferrata* were mobilised to respond to the attack from Jewish insurgents. Archaeology suggests a dramatic response to the emergency. A group of Roman soldiers was apparently ordered to go with their entrenching tools to the base's headquarters (*principia*). There stood an over-life-size bronze statue of Hadrian, shown wearing a commander's panoply. The finely crafted head may have been cast in a workshop in Rome and brought to Iudaea by the legion when it relocated to the Beth Shean Valley. (It may have served a ritual function there, perhaps either standing outside in the courtyard or inside the building surrounded by the legion's insignia.) The condition of the head and torso – though missing the arms and legs – when it was found in modern times strongly suggests that it was buried in the ground by Roman legionaries to prevent it from falling into enemy hands and being defaced. The camp then seems to have been evacuated.

As intelligence reports of the uprising reached Caesarea, Rufus learned the name of his Jewish adversary. The garbled spellings in the later historical accounts hint that the first Roman army clerks to hear the unfamiliar Hebrew name struggled to transcribe it into Latin or Greek, reporting it variously as 'Cochebas' (Eusebius, *Chronicle*) or 'Bar Chocheba' (Justin quoted by Eusebius, *Church History* 4.8), or 'Bar Chochabas' (Jerome, *The Apology Against the Books of Rufinus*). The moniker Bar Kokhba had already superseded the man's real name.

The role of Rabbi Akiba in declaring the rebel leader as 'King Messiah' may have been the real reason behind his arrest by the Roman authorities, likely in AD 132 (though a later date is possible). His actual involvement in the Bar Kokhba War cannot now be determined. According to Jewish

This is a Roman bronze coin overstruck by the rebel administration during the first year of independence (AD 132/133). The obverse shows a palm branch within a wreath, and the legend 'Shim'on Prince of Israel' reading anti-clockwise in paleo-Hebrew characters. The reverse shows a six-stringed instrument (*chelys*) and the inscription announces 'Year 1 of the Redemption of Israel'. (Classical Numismatics Group, www.cngcoins.com)

tradition, he was seized for continuing to teach Torah publicly, which had been outlawed on pain of death. He was sentenced by Rufus to die. As he faced his execution in Caesarea on the eve of Yom Kippur, Akiba recited the Shema (one of two daily prayers specified in the Torah, beginning 'Hear, Israel, the Lord is our God'). The venerable rabbi uttered his prayer calmly, even as he suffered terrible agonies from being flayed. Perplexed by his serenity, Rufus asked him whether he was a sorcerer, since he appeared to feel no pain. Akiba replied: 'I am neither a sorcerer nor a mocker, but I rejoice at the opportunity now given to me to love my God "with all my life," seeing that I have hitherto been able to love Him only "with all my means" and "with all my might"' (Jerusalem Talmud 9.14b). He then recited a verse from Torah and uttered the words: 'Behold the cause of my joy' – and with that he expired.

WAR OF ATTRITION

At the end of the first combat season Tineius Rufus reflected soberly on his situation. He had failed to regain control of his province. Despite having two legions and several auxiliary cohorts at his disposal the rebels had seized a large tract of territory – and were holding on to it. It was every governor's nightmare. He needed to redouble his counterinsurgency efforts and he needed more troops to replace the casualties his army had already sustained.

This was likely the time Rufus appealed for help from Hadrian. A hostile state could not be allowed to establish itself within Rome's dominions or sphere of influence. Its geography would rip a hole in the integrity of the eastern Mediterranean. It must be surrounded and obliterated. The emperor, understanding the need for containment and a swift end to the troubles, responded to the request by authorizing deployment of additional units from the military commands in the neighbouring provinces. 'Then, indeed,' writes Cassius Dio, 'Hadrian sent against them his best generals' (*Roman History* 69.13.2). Initially detachments (*vexillationes*) composed of cohorts – rather

'Soon all Iudaea had been stirred up,' writes Cassius Dio (*Roman History* 69.13.1). Roman troops sent by Tineius Rufus to contain and extinguish the rebellion were impeded in their progress by the absence of military roads in large tracts of terrain. In the vales of the Judaean Hills, the Jews had the advantage. (Author's collection)

AMBUSH IN TEKOA (PP. 48–49)

Along with two legions stationed in the province of Iudaea were at least two cohorts of professional non-citizen auxiliary troops, including the *Cohors I Miliaria Thracum*, which was encamped at Beit Guvrin. In this reconstruction, a detachment of Roman auxiliary infantrymen on a routine patrol is ambushed in a street of Tekoa.

The village lay within the rebel jurisdiction of Herodium. Taking control of this and other villages early in the revolt would help secure the region, which was the military and administrative centre of Shim'on ben Koseba's new Jewish state. Famous as having been home to the shepherd Amos of the Old Testament, Tekoa was located 19km (12 miles – or a day's march) south of Jerusalem – the city the rebels hoped ultimately to liberate from the Romans.

Trained for fighting on an open battlefield, in an urban environment these Roman auxiliary infantrymen **(1)** are at a disadvantage when faced with an organized guerrilla insurgency. They wear bronze helmets, giving good protection from blows to the head from above or the side. Their chain-mail suits, made of thousands of iron links riveted together, are designed to withstand slashes or stabs from bladed weapons. The flat oval shields can be used both defensively (to block handheld weapons and deflect missiles) and offensively (to punch an opponent with the shield boss or strike him with the blunt edge). In the confined space, however, they cannot use their spears effectively.

In contrast, the men **(2)** of the local Jewish militia know well their enemies' weaknesses. Dressed to blend in with the villagers, they use the element of surprise to surround and overwhelm the unsuspecting Roman soldiers. Equipped with knives **(3)**, they slit the enemies' unprotected throats from behind, or shoot them with arrows fired from bows from afar. Afterwards they can retrieve the Roman arms and armour to equip their own growing army of resistance.

Similar attacks were carried out in towns and villages all across the Judaean Hills and Judaean Shephelah at the start of the Bar Kokhba War in AD 132 and into 133. The historian Cassius Dio writes that the Romans were somewhat dismissive of reports of the initial assaults. 'Soon, however, all Judaea had been stirred up,' he records, 'and the Jews everywhere were showing signs of disturbance' (*Roman History* 56.13.1). At the end of the first year, Tineius Rufus, *Legatus Augusti Pro Praetore* of Iudaea, found himself firmly on the defensive.

A *shekel* struck by the rebel administration during the second year of independence (AD 133–134) displays the façade of the Temple and a showbread table within, a star (*kohav*) above and the name Shim'on on the sides. The reverse shows agricultural symbols associated with the harvest festival of Sukkot: a *lulav* (frond of the date palm) with an *ethrog* (yellow citron) on the left. The accompanying inscription announces 'Year 2 of the Freedom of Israel'. (Classical Numismatics Group, www.cngcoins.com)

than entire legions – marched from their base camps along the roadways of the empire to the war zone. From the north *Legio* III *Gallica* arrived. In the column was the *Legatus Augusti Pro Praetore* of Syria, C. Quinctius Certus Publicius Marcellus. Confident that the Jews were not a problem in his own province he had left Ti. Severus (the legate of *Legio* IIII *Scythica*) in charge. From Egypt a vexillation of *Legio* II *Traiana* arrived.

From Arabia Petraea in the east, III *Cyrenaica* reached Iudaea with its provincial commander, T. Haterius Nepos. For the moment, the Jews in his province posed no threat, and any (like Babatha) who were sympathetic to the rebels had already departed for Iudaea. It was a calculated gamble, however. III *Cyrenaica* was the only legion in Arabia Petraea. Its withdrawal might put the province at risk if the mood of the resident Jews changed. One scholar has proposed that, in fact, the Jews in Arabia took advantage of the rebellion in Iudaea and *did* rise up. If so, Nepos then authorized a massacre of Jews, which was the cause of Babatha's flight. The evidence, however, is inconclusive.

The infusion added up to 11,200 more combatants to check the contagion and prevent it from spreading. With the additional resources the Romans launched a new campaign in AD 133: 'As the rebellion of the Jews at this time grew much more serious, Rufus, governor of Iudea, after an auxiliary force had been sent him by the emperor, using their madness as a pretext, proceeded against them without mercy, and destroyed indiscriminately thousands of men and women and children' (Eusebius, *Church History* 4.6).

Ben Koseba's strategy was working – and very effectively too. His rebel army continued to resist Roman attempts to regain control. Inspired by their early victories, when the army of Israel went into battle the soldiers shouted: 'O God, neither help nor discourage us!' (Midrash Rabbah, *Lamentations* 2.2.4). His men continued to excavate tunnels and underground hideouts from which they launched more attacks, and in which they stored additional weapons that they had amassed from the fallen Romans, or made themselves.

Probably still commanding operations from his base at Herodium, Ben Koseba needed more soldiers to replace his casualties. It is recorded

By AD 134–135 'the war reached its height' (Eusebius, *Church History* 4.6). Taking command of operations, Sex. Iulius Severus implemented a new counterinsurgency strategy. With outside resources supplementing the resident provincial units, the Romans began to recapture territory by focusing efforts on small targets (like Horvat Zalit and Horvat 'Ethri), surrounding them and starving them into submission. This new approach also reduced the risk of casualties to the Roman side. (Author's collection)

The fortified village of Horvat 'Ethri, on a hill 406m above sea level, combined domestic dwellings with public buildings, all arranged around a central courtyard. One of the structures has been interpreted to be a synagogue. The village was damaged in the First Jewish War, but was restored in the years preceding the Bar Kokhba War, during which it was a rebel stronghold. (Ganot, Wikimedia Commons, CC-BY-SA-3.0)

that Akiba's students had been struck down with plague and many had died from it. According to tradition the turning point was the 33rd day of the Counting of the Omer (*Lag B'Omer*) on the 18th day of the month of *Iyyar*. (An *omer* is a sheaf of barley, and this festival is held at the time of the barley harvest in May). The dying stopped. Other men responded voluntarily to the call to action. Success is a great attractor of support. News of the rebels' victories even drew support from beyond Iudaea. Cassius Dio writes: 'many outside nations, too, were joining them through eagerness for gain, and the whole earth, one might almost say, was being stirred up over the matter' (*Roman History* 69.13.2). Among them were mercenaries from Nabataea, attracted to the conflict not by glory, but cash and a share of war spoils. The Christian community, however, adamantly refused to assist him. Ben Koseba now showed a cruel and vindictive side to his nature. If they were not for him, he determined that they were against him. In his description of the key events of the second year of the war Eusebius remarks: 'Cochebas, *dux* (leader) of the Jewish sect, killed the Christians with all kinds of persecutions [when] they refused to help him against the Roman troops.' (Hadrian's Year 17, *Chronicle*).

While the Romans stepped up their offensive, the insurgents proved able to match them. The Midrash tells one apocryphal tale of Jewish valour:

> There were two brothers in Kefar Haruba, who did not allow any Roman to pass there, because they killed him. They said: 'The conclusion of the whole matter is that we must take Hadrian's crown and set it upon our own head.' They heard that the Romans were coming towards them; and when they set out against them, an old man met them and said: 'May the Creator be your help against them!' They retorted: 'Let him neither help nor discourage us!' (Midrash Rabbah, *Lamentations* 2.2.4)

The Jews may even have succeeded in destroying an entire Roman legion. *Legio* XXII *Deiotariana* is known to have been based in Egypt in AD 119 (or 123), yet it is missing from an inscription carved in the time of M.

Aurelius (AD 161–180), which lists all legions then in service. Its absence from the later inscription implies that it had been disbanded or annihilated in the intervening years. One explanation – which is disputed – is that the legion was destroyed in the Bar Kokhba War. It was not reconstituted.

At times, even when not engaged in combat, the two sides were physically very close to each other. An epistolary affadavit (a combination letter-legal document) was written on behalf of both of the *parnasim* of Beth Mashiko to Yeshua ben Galgula, the *rosh hamahanaya* at Herodium. In it they explained that a soldier unlawfully took a cow from a resident of the village, named Ya'akob ben Yehudah, who had purchased it, and the administrators claimed back the animal on the man's behalf. The claimants sought to explain they could not petition Ben Galgula in person because 'the Gentiles are near us' (*P. Mur* 42) – in other words, units of Roman soldiers were stationed in the vicinity and it was too dangerous for the claimant and all the witnesses to travel beyond the village. The scribe, Ya'akob ben Yosef, who was also a militiaman, went alone and delivered it by hand to Ben Galgula at command headquarters in Herodium. Ensuring that the rule of law prevailed in the Land of Israel was important.

Cassius Dio records that the Jews 'might meet together unobserved underground' (*Roman History*, 69.12.3). Beneath the fortified village of Horvat Burgin the inhabitants excavated burrows in the living rock. The defenders could hide themselves here, as well as store provender and military *matériel*. (Deror avi, Wikimedia Commons, CC-BY-SA-3.0)

That the civilian population felt their lives were relatively secure under their Jewish administrations around Iudaea is illustrated by surviving contracts which document the buying or leasing of land and property. In the spring of that year Eleazar ben Shmuel paid 650 *zuzim* to lease land in Ein Gedi. He proceeded to make the initial payment on the negotiated lease in the autumn.

The government of Ben Koseba celebrated its survival into a second year with new issues of coins. More Roman silver *denarii* or *drachmae* were converted into Jewish *zuzim*. In one type, a palm branch decorating

A silver *shekel* struck by the rebel administration during the third year of independence (AD 134–135) displays the façade of the Temple and the holy Ark of the Covenant within, a star above and the name Shim'on on the sides in paleo-Hebrew characters. The reverse shows a *lulav* with *ethrog* on the left and the inscription announces 'For the Freedom of Jerusalem'. (Roma Numismatics, www.romanumismatics.com)

A silver *zuz* struck by the rebel administration during the third year of independence (AD 134–135) displays a bunch of grapes and the name Shim'on on the sides in paleo-Hebrew characters. The reverse shows a palm branch and the inscription announces 'For the Freedom of Jerusalem'. (Roma Numismatics, www.romanumismatics.com)

the centre of the flan is framed by the Hebrew legend 'Year Two of the Freedom of Israel', while the other side shows three bunches of grapes hanging from a branch and the name of the war leader 'Shim'on'. A lower-value bronze coin shows a palm branch within a wreath and Hebrew inscription 'Shim'on Prince of Israel' on one side, and on the other a wide lyre of four strings surrounded by the slogan 'Year Two of the Freedom of Israel'.

Coins minted by the rebel regime would only be used by sellers and buyers willing to accept them as legal tender. The presence of such coins in the archaeological record is an indicator of the whereabouts of people and places sympathetic to the insurgents. The coins have been found as far north-west as Horvat Burnat (near Lod), north-east as far as Wadi ed-Daliyeh (north of Jericho), west as far as Kibbutz Gak (near Beit Guvrin) and south as far as En Boqeq. The new Land of Israel thus encompassed the foothills, mountains and deserts of Iudaea and Benjamin. The paucity of coins found in Jerusalem, Galilee or Transjordan strongly suggests that Ben Koseba's rebellion did not include these regions.

Despite the presence of several legions and auxiliary cohorts, progress in clawing back territory from the rebels was achingly slow. An indication of the gravity of the situation is preserved by Cassius Dio: 'Hadrian in writing to the Senate did not employ the opening phrase commonly affected by the emperors, "If you and our children are in health, it is well; I and the legions are in health"' (*Roman History* 69.14.3).

A new approach was needed. Joining the leadership team in the war theatre was Q. Lollius Urbicus, who was in charge of *Legio* X *Gemina* stationed in Pannonia Superior, and named as 'legate of Commander Hadrian' (*legatus imperatoris Hadriani*). About his war plan nothing is recorded, though his contribution would later be recognized.

However, one man who is singled out for particular mention by Cassius Dio is Iulius Severus. He was then *Legatus Augusti Pro Praetore* of Britannia. Hadrian ordered him to march to Iudaea without delay. On the long journey Severus may have been accompanied by detachments of men from his own province: *Legio* XX *Valeria Victrix* from Deva (Chester) – among whom was centurion Q. Albius Felix; VI *Victrix* from Eboracum (York); and the auxiliary units *Cohors* I *Hispanorum* (Maryport) under M. Censorius Cornelianus as *praepositus*, and *Cohors* IV *Lingonum*. How the military reporting structure now worked in Iudaea after he arrived is not understood.

Judaea Campaign, AD 134–136

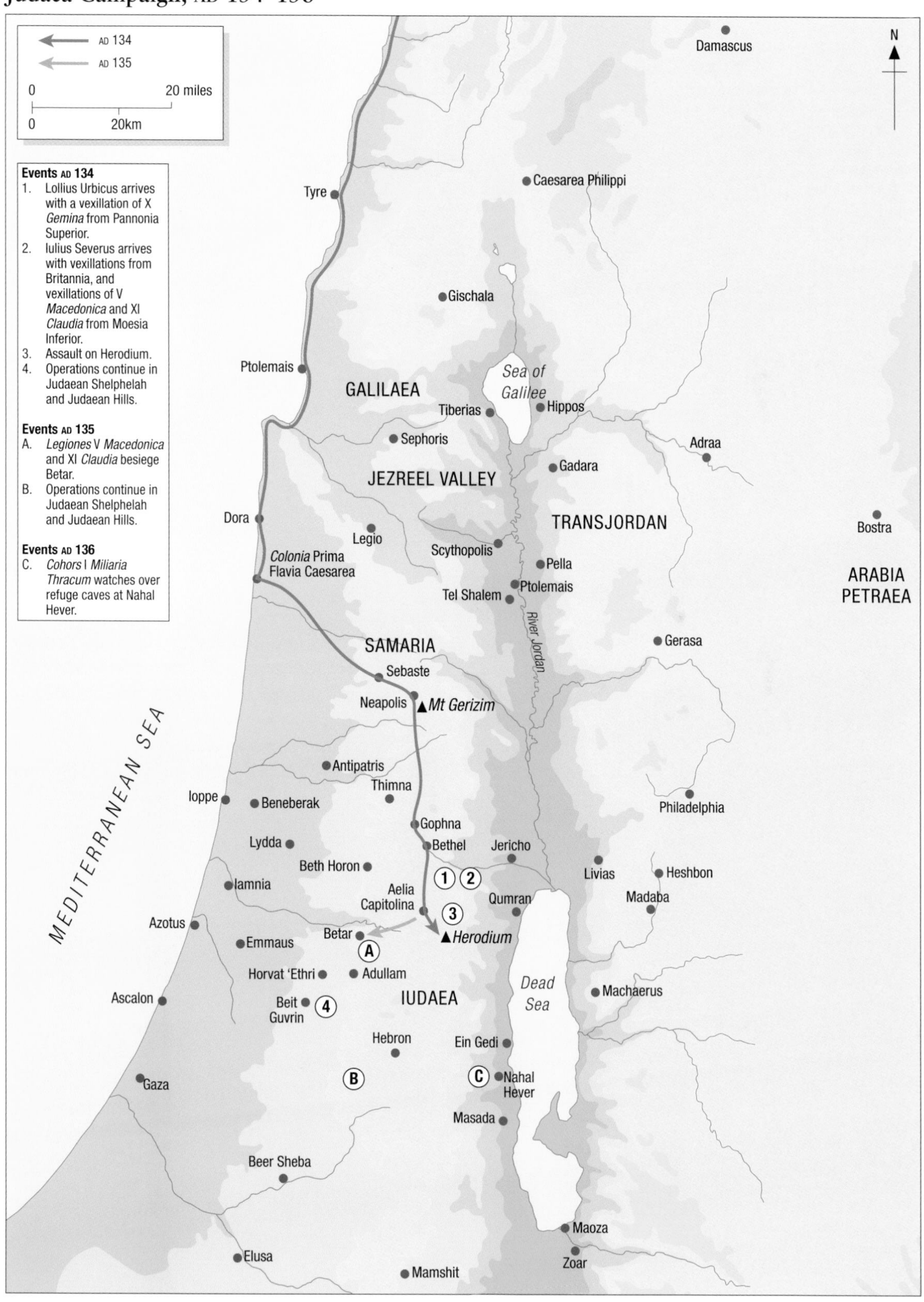

A silver *zuz* struck by the rebel administration during the third year of independence (AD 134–135) displays a bunch of grapes and the name Shim'on on the sides in paleo-Hebrew characters. The reverse shows a three-stringed *kithara* and the inscription announces 'For the Freedom of Israel'. (Roma Numismatics, www.romanumismatics.com. Coin in author's collection)

Severus may have been placed in overall command of military operations, which would have subordinated the host governor Rufus along with the other legates. Alternatively all guest commanders might have retained their ranks and reported to Rufus as the military governor of Iudaea for the duration of the war; or Severus and Rufus could have worked together with the other legates as equals. It is unclear if Hadrian went to Iudaea to direct operations in person.

TURNING POINT

The following year (AD 134) 'the war reached its height' (Eusebius, *Church History* 4.6). There were now soldiers of up to 12 legions in action in Iudaea. Augmenting the forces of VI *Ferrata* and X *Fretensis* already based in Iudaea was III *Gallica* (in its entirety) from Syria, as well as vexillations: III *Cyrenaica* from Arabia Petraea; II *Traiana Fortis* (and perhaps XXII *Deiotoriana*) from Egypt; XII *Fulminata* from Cappadocia; V *Macedonica* and XI *Claudia* from

Depicted on Trajan's Column is the mobile *carroballista*, a catapult on a two-wheeled cart pulled by a donkey or mule. Tests with modern reconstructions show that Roman catapults were sufficiently accurate over 365m (1,200ft) that an experienced team of gunners could hit specific targets, and reload the piece every 15–20 seconds. (Public domain)

Caves in Judaea

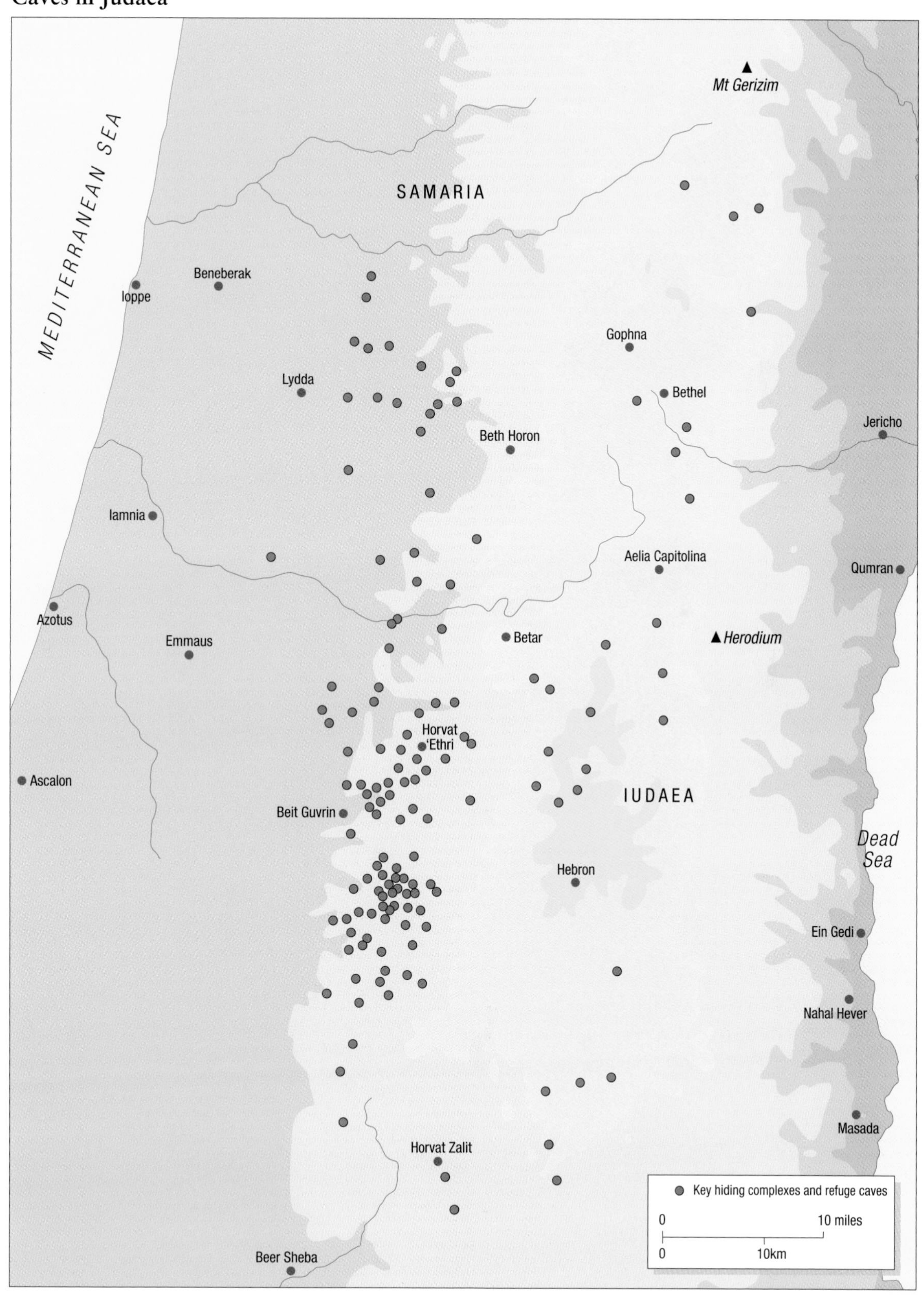

ASSAULT ON HORVAT 'ETHRI FORTIFIED VILLAGE (PP. 58–59)

In the first phase of the war, the Romans tried to engage the rebels on the open battlefield. However, Shim'on ben Koseba's troops avoided set-piece battles at all costs and, instead, employed the tactics of the insurgent to ambush Roman troops on the march. When Iulius Severus, *Legatus Augusti Pro Praetore* of the province of Britannia (operating on the direct instructions of Emperor Hadrian) arrived in AD 134, he changed the campaign's military strategy. He took the fight to the Jews in their homes.

In this reconstruction, a detachment of Roman legionaries attacks the fortified hilltop farm at Horvat 'Ethri in AD 134. The Romans have penetrated one of the entrances and progressed into the complex, comprising a cluster of buildings surrounding a courtyard. The Jews have been forced onto the defensive. Standing on rooftops **(1)** and in the side streets below **(2)** they lob sling stones or fire arrows at the approaching Romans. In the middle distance legionaries advance in *testudo* or tortoise formation **(3)**, with shields raised and interlocked to protect themselves from the missiles raining down upon them.

In the foreground, a Roman centurion **(4)**, who led the offensive, has been struck down by an arrow. Surrounded by men of his *centuria,* who have raised their shields to protect him, he is attended by a *capsarius* **(5)**, a medic trained in first aid. By Hadrian's time Roman medical practice has developed techniques, instruments and medications for a wide range of battle traumas. Cleaning the wound is an important first step to recovery, followed by dressing it with a bandage; and 'if it is not effective when dry,' writes A. Cornelius Celsus (*c.* 25 BC to *c.* AD 50) the Roman encyclopaedist, 'it is to be soaked in vinegar. Vinegar is powerful in suppressing a flow of blood; and some, therefore, pour it into wounds' (*On Medicine* 5.21).

Severus' strategy change worked: 'he was able, rather slowly, to be sure, but with comparatively little danger, to crush, exhaust and exterminate them,' writes Cassius Dio, who notes 'very few of them in fact survived' (*Roman History* 56.13.3). Nevertheless, the Bar Kokhba War saw heavy Roman casualties overall that were still talked about decades after the conflict's end. The Roman grammarian, rhetorician and advocate M. Cornelius Fronto (*c.* AD 100 to late 160s) wrote to the then Emperor Marcus Aurelius: 'under the rule of your grandfather Hadrian what a number of soldiers were killed by the Jews!' (*Letters, On the Parthian War* AD 162).

Moesia Inferior; X *Gemina* from Pannonia Superior; and now (possibly) VI *Victrix* and XX *Valeria Victrix* from Britannia. Supporting them were several auxiliary *alae*, *cohortes* and mixed units. It was a heavy investment in blood and treasure by Hadrian, but a necessary one to break the usurper's hold on Iudaea.

Jewish insurgents improvised weapons and repurposed old ones. This spear actually consists of an iron tip from a bolt used with a Roman catapult, re-attached to a new wooden shaft. It was found in the Cave of Figs, Judaean Desert. (Exhibit at the Israel Museum, Jerusalem. Author's collection)

Severus joined the war effort at a crucial time. It had taken two years to make any kind of progress. Working against the Romans was the large number of enemy combatants and their use of underground hideouts and fortified strongholds. From now on the Romans adopted a cautious, but steady, strategy of divide and conquer: 'Severus did not venture to attack his opponents in the open at any one point, in view of their numbers and their desperation, but by intercepting small groups, thanks to the number of his soldiers and his under-officers, and by depriving them of food and shutting them up, he was able, rather slowly, to be sure, but with comparatively little danger, to crush, exhaust and exterminate them' (Cassius Dio, *Roman History* 69.13.3).

From the watchtower at Horvat Zalit the lookout sounded the alarm. The tower, surrounded by a glacis, stood on a spur overlooking Nahal Eshtemo'a on the southern slopes of the Judaean Shephelah (about 1.5km (1 mile) south-east of modern Meitar). From this high vantage point he could see the Roman army coming. In the courtyard and surrounding rooms below, the Jews stopped what they were doing and prepared to defend themselves. Archaeologists working at the site in 1983 and 1984 found a coin hoard with Roman coins as well as overstamped examples. They believe the place may have served as a mint producing coins for the rebel administration and that the coin maker was interrupted and hurriedly stashed the pile, intending to recover it later.

Some 32km (20 miles) to the north at Kirbet 'Ethri near Beit Guvrin another fortified courtyard settlement faced the imminent arrival of the Roman army. It had been destroyed during the First Jewish War, but in the intervening years half of the old complex had been restored and new features added. Some buildings now rose to two storeys. One room likely served the community as a synagogue. Below ground the new inhabitants had dug out burrows and chambers connected by tunnels. The subterranean complex had been designed with war in mind. It was accessible through vertical or stepped shafts carved into the bedrock floors of the rooms. Recesses at the heads of the shafts accommodated blocks of stone designed to conceal the entrances.

When the Romans stormed the place the occupants fought back, but they were unable to repel the enemy. Archaeologists working at the site from 1999 to 2001 found a burnt layer at the centre of the site at floor level – evidence of an extensive fire. A rebel *zuz* of the Ben Koseba regime, which showed scorch marks, was found in the layer, confirming the date as contemporary with the Bar Kokhba War. The ritual bath (*mikwa*) of the settlement had been used as a makeshift burial. It contained the skulls and bones of at least 12 individuals (seven adults, including females and males, four adolescents and one foetus). They had apparently all been slaughtered during the capture of the settlement. Cut marks on a neck vertebra were found during conservation, indicating that at least one individual had been beheaded by the blow of a sword. The bones also showed evidence that they had been left exposed in the open air for a while, no doubt where they began to decompose in the heat. Only later were the corpses gathered up and unceremoniously buried in the *mikwa*, lying among the ephemera of everyday life – bowls, casseroles, cooking pots, jars, jugs and oil-lamps. Two silver coins had fused together and some of the glass vessels had deformed in the intense heat when the buildings were set alight.

All over the Judaean Shephelah and Judaean Hills the same grim process of pacification was executed with unrelenting efficiency. What role *Classis Syriacae* – the navy unit in Syria at Seleucia Pieria – played is nowhere explained in the accounts which survive. That it did play a role is suggested by an inscription honouring its equestrian prefect. It may have provided vessels to transport troops from Britannia, Moesia Inferior and Pannonia Superior from embarkation points by sea to Caesarea or Yoppe. It may have patrolled the Dead Sea, intercepting and blockading supplies moving in and out of Ein Gedi. (A wooden anchor, which originally weighed 130kg (286lb), made from a jujube tree, reinforced with lead, iron and bronze with some of its ropes still attached, and dated to the Roman period, was found at Ein Gedi in 2005.) Alternatively, its marines may have joined the land army as a fighting force in its own right, replacing Roman casualties, which were running high. It has also been suggested that men of the fleet at Misenum were transferred to Iudaea to join *Legio* X *Fretensis*, but the documentary evidence is open to interpretation.

Yet away from the myriad battlefields, life in the Judaean hinterland carried on. The Jewish population still felt secure under their joint civil and military administrations. From the autumn of that year Eleazar ben Shmuel

Located on a hill in the Rephaim Valley, 11km (7 miles) south-west of Jerusalem, Betar was the site of Ben Koseba's last stand. Part of the defensive circuit wall, which was hurriedly erected when the Romans arrived to besiege the city, still survives at Khirbet el-Yahud near Bittir. (Bukvoed, Wikimedia Commons, CC-BY-SA-4.0)

Refuge Caves, Judaean Desert

and his friends together shared fields. In the winter Hillel ben Garis leased land in Ir-Nahash, while Yehudah ben Yehudah borrowed one *tetradrachma* (a coin worth four *drachmae*).

Celebrating its third year, the government of Ben Koseba minted new issues of coins, though from now on it omitted the number of anniversaries. In one type a wreath surrounds the name of 'Shim'on', while the opposite side shows a flagon with a handle and the words 'For the Freedom of Jerusalem'. On another coin the façade of the Temple at Jerusalem is depicted, its doors open with a showbread table inside, and a star above, all flanked by letters spelling the name 'Shim'on'. Paired on the other side is a *lulav* (a closed frond of the date palm tree) and an *etrog* (a fruit used in the rituals of the festival of Sukkot) with the familiar message 'For the Freedom of Jerusalem'. Yet the harsh truth for the rebel leader and his followers was that Jerusalem had remained firmly in Roman control the whole time. The Temple was not yet built and it was becoming painfully evident to many supporting the King Messiah that it never would be. Yet hope of achieving it remained a driving force for leader Ben Koseba.

Maintaining the commitment, cohesion and discipline among his militia units was now of primary concern to Ben Koseba. Without their continued support the rebel state would quickly collapse. He took a close and personal interest in matters. At his command centre at Betar he dictated a confidential letter to a scribe in Aramaic:

> Letter of Shimeon ben Koseba, peace!
> To Yehonathan, son of Be'ayan: [My order is] that whatever Elisha tells you, do to him and help him and those with him [or: in every action].
> Be well.
> (*P. Yadin* 53)

Perhaps Elisha was planning an important mission and Yehonathan had a special skill he could use to help him accomplish it?

Binding them all together in common cause was their Jewish faith. As Prince Over Israel by official title and redeeming King Messiah by rabbinic interpretation, he actively encouraged religious observance among the militias:

> Shimeon to Yehudah bar Menashe in Kiryat 'Arabaya. I have sent to you two donkeys, and you must send with them two men to Yehonathan, son of Be'ayan and to Masabala, in order that they shall pack and send to the camp, towards you, palm branches and citrons. And you, from your place, send others who will bring you myrtles and willows. See that they are tithed and send them to the camp. The request is made because the army is big. Be well.
> (*P. Yadin* 57)

In making this request he was invoking the command in the Torah: 'And you shall take you on the first day the boughs of goodly trees, branches of palm trees, and the boughs of thick trees, and willows of the brook; and ye shall rejoice before the Lord your God seven days' (*Leviticus* 23:40). The letter hints at the growing uncertainty of the current circumstances. Ben Koseba had to provide the means to transport the items because the men in Kiryat

Approaching a fortified stronghold was a high-risk mission. The *testudo* offered a group of soldiers protection from the defenders' missiles raining down from above. The front row of soldiers interlocked their shields to form a wall, while those behind held theirs above their heads like a tortoise shell. By co-ordinating the footwork the formation could be remarkably agile. (Public domain)

'Arabaya presumably did not have pack animals available to spare. It also implies that if he did not send the donkeys the militia might not carry out the order.

At the start of AD 135 the pressure on Ben Koseba was now severe. His 'big army' had suffered terrible casualties and what was left was struggling to resist the Roman onslaught. Aggravating the situation was that some of his remaining regional militias were flouting their obligations to support their fellow soldiers. In a letter to the *rosh hamahanaya* on the Dead Sea he writes angrily:

> From Shimeon ben Koseba to the men of En-gedi. To Masabala and to Yehonathan bar Be'ayan, peace! In comfort you sit, eat and drink from the property of the House of Israel, and care nothing for your brothers.
> (*P. Yadin* 49)

Some camp commanders seemed willing to ignore his orders altogether:

> Shimeon ben Koseba to Yehonathan and to Masabala... Let all men from Tekoa and other places who are with you, be sent to me without delay. And if you shall not send them, let it be known to you, that you will be punished...
> (*P. Yadin* 55)

Embedded with civilians and away from the front, perhaps the soldiery did not appreciate the gravity of their worsening predicament. Several men gathered in a scribe's shop in Ein Gedi to sign an agreement about sharing fields with Eleazar ben Shmuel on 'the twenty-eighth *Marcheshvan* of the Third Year of Shim'on ben Koseba, Prince Over Israel' (*P. Yadin* 44), which dates the document to 6 November AD 134. He also invested in a house in Kfar Baarou – something Shaul ben he-Harash and Eleazar ha-Shoter felt comfortable doing as well. Indeed, Eleazar ben Levi bought several houses and a courtyard. They evidently believed in the long-term viability of the revolution and were investing their cash based on that belief, but for others it was speculation. The price of property had fallen. Those with ready cash could buy houses at a discount and make money from rents. While the economy of Ein Gedi remained robust, the reality was that the future of Israel was very far from certain.

LAST STAND AT BETAR

Despite three years of determined resistance, Hadrian's army was proving itself successful at retaking large areas of the Judaean Shephelah and Judaean Desert from the rebels. When and how Herodium fell is nowhere recorded: the carefully dug secret tunnels did not, in the end, prevent its capture from an army practised in siege warfare. Roman units remained in the reconquered region to ensure the Jewish insurgents caused no further harm. The tide had turned. Eusebius writes: 'no high tower, no fortified wall, no mightiest navy and not the most diligent in commerce could overcome the might of the Roman army; and the citizens of Iudaea came to such distress that they, together with their wives, their children, their gold and their silver, in which they trusted, remained in underground tunnels and deepest caves' (*On Isaiah* 2:15).

The rest of the expeditionary force under Severus' command now turned its attention east to the Judaean Hills. The Romans had identified Betar as the centre of the rebels' operations. It was a strategic imperative that Betar be captured and Ben Koseba taken – either alive (so he could be displayed in triumph by Hadrian) or dead (bringing an end to his claim to be the king messiah). Two legions struck out from the rest to take the target. By the summer, *Legio* V *Macedonica* and XI *Claudia* had arrived at the rebel-held town.

The town lay on a hill (nowadays called Khirbet el-Yahud), 700m (2,300ft) above sea level, in the Rephaim Valley. It was located 11km (7 miles) south-west of Jerusalem on the Roman road to Gaza, and just 24km (15 miles) north-east of Horvat 'Ethri. The hilltop sloped gradually to the north to the steep drop of the Nahal Sorek 150m (490ft) above the valley floor. The town itself was reached by a rock-cut approach road on the south-eastern side. The inhabitants were supplied with water from a spring in the valley below and likely one or more cisterns or caves cut into the rock. Archaeologists estimate the pre-war population of the unwalled town of 10 acres (4 hectares) was between 1,000 and 2,000 people. Since AD 132 it had steadily filled with Jews fleeing the advancing Roman army. Three years later it must have looked like a shanty town, with every available space between the existing buildings occupied by temporary shacks and tents. The Babylonian Talmud records: 'There were 400 synagogues in the city of Betar, and

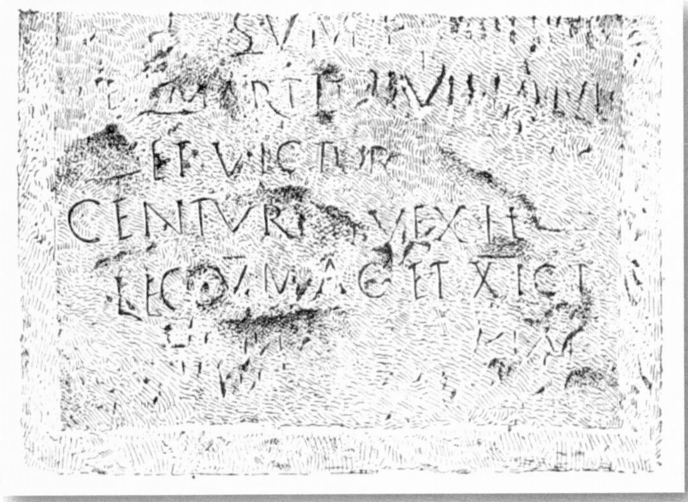

An inscription found beside the freshwater spring at Betar in the Rephaim Valley confirms the presence of vexillations of *Legiones* V *Macedonica* and XI *Claudia*. These units had marched from Moesia Inferior to the war zone. The illustration is in Charles Clermont-Ganneau's *Archaeological Researches in Palestine During the Years 1873–74*. (Public domain)

in every one were 400 teachers of children, and each one had under him 400 pupils' (*Gittin* 58a). The numbers are undoubtedly exaggerated, but they do convey the sense of the town being overwhelmed by refugees. Among the civilians were men of Ben Koseba's army. The Babylonian Talmud states: 'eighty [thousand] battle trumpets assembled in the city of Betar' (*Gittin* 57a) – almost certainly a grossly inflated number of soldiers, but nevertheless confirmation that armed Jewish troops were at Betar in some strength.

The legions set up their camps on the south-east side overlooking Betar. What followed was a Roman textbook siege. Below in the valley floor soldiers located the spring and set up a picket to prevent the rebels from replenishing their store of water. Without water the rebels would not be able to withstand a blockade for long. Meanwhile the other soldiers erected a siege wall or circumvallation of field-stones – a 'fence consisting of the slain' (Midrash Rabbah, *Lamentations* 2.2.4) – to seal off the town. Its inhabitants could not now get out without risk of capture and relief troops coming to their rescue could not get in. Unlike at Masada there is no evidence of a ramp for a siege tower.

Ben Koseba responded by erecting a stout but roughly finished stone wall around the town. In constructing the wall they had to demolish several existing buildings in a few places in order to create a continuous line following the contours of the hill. The Jews used recycled material (such as prepared ashlar blocks from the Herodian-era buildings they had pulled down) in their new structure, the purpose of which was entirely defensive. The jerry-built construction hints at the speed at which the besieged army of Israel had to raise it. Semi-circular buttresses and rectangular external towers were set at intervals along the south and west sides – at least six semi-circular towers and three square ones. Eusebius describes the resulting stronghold as 'a very secure fortress' (*Church History*, 4.3). Within the wall, defenders chipped rocks (flint or limestone) to make round slingstones – ranging in size from 5cm to 9cm, and in weight from 110g to 650g (4oz to 23oz) – and kept them beside the new circuit wall. They also amassed iron arrows in preparation for the expected attack.

The mood inside the citadel was tense. The Jewish sources portray the commander-in-chief as a *gibbor*:

> In the city was Rabbi Eleazar of Modi'in, who continually wore sackcloth and fasted, and used to pray daily: 'Lord of the universe, sit not in judgment today!' so that Hadrian thought of returning home.
>
> A Cuthean went [to the Roman emperor] and found him and said: 'My lord, so long as that old cock wallows in ashes, you will not conquer the city. But wait for me, because I will do something that will enable you to subdue it to-day.'
>
> He immediately entered the gate of the city, where he found Rabbi Eleazar standing and praying. He pretended to whisper in the ear of Rabbi Eleazar of Modi'in. People went and informed Bar Koseba: 'Your friend, Rabbi Eleazar, wishes to surrender the city to Hadrian.'
>
> He sent and had the Cuthean brought to him and asked: 'What did you say to him?'
>
> He replied: 'If I tell you, the emperor will kill me; and if I do not tell you, you will kill me. It is better that I should kill myself and the secrets of the government be not divulged.'

JEWISH FORCES

A. 4,000–8,000 men under Shim'on ben Koseba

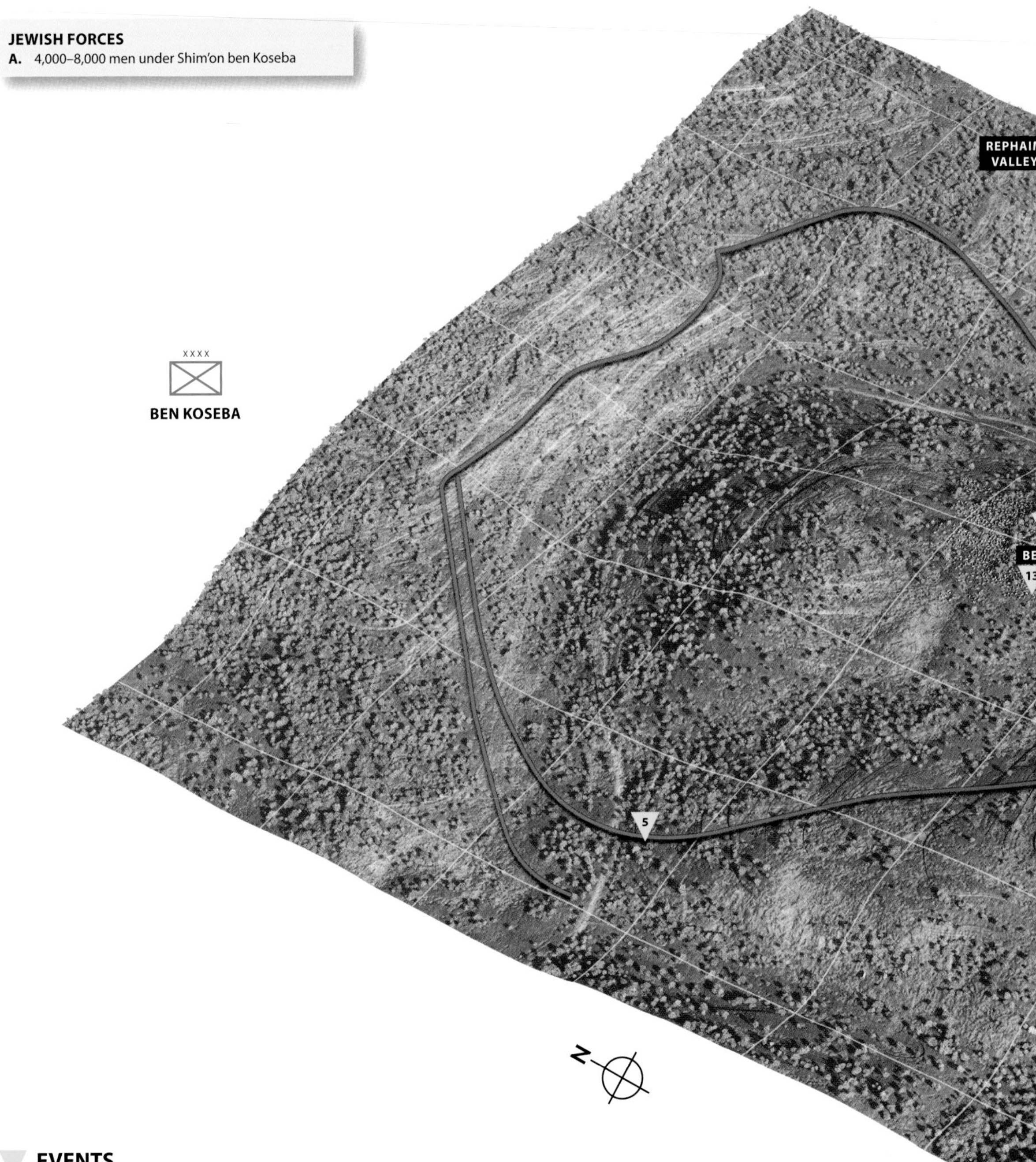

EVENTS

1. Shimo'n ben Koseba establishes his headquarters at Betar. Refugees fleeing the Roman army advancing through the Judaean Shephelah and Judaean Hills settle in the increasingly crowded city.

2. Vexillations of *Legiones* V *Macedonica* and XI *Claudia* arrive in the Rephaim Valley, establishing camps on the crest of the southern range of hills opposite Betar.

3. A legionary picket is placed around the spring in the base of the valley to prevent the Jewish rebels from accessing it.

4. Ben Koseba orders a wall to be erected around the town. When existing buildings stand on the plotted course of the wall they are pulled down. Material from the demolished buildings is incorporated in the roughly constructed wall, buttressed by circular bastions.

5. Legionaries erect a circumvallation over the crest of the surrounding hills using field stones to prevent the insurgents from escaping and any relief troops attempting to enter Betar.

6. Defenders inside Betar shape flint and limestone into slingstones.

7. Legionaries assemble at the base of the hill in readiness for the final assault.

8. According to Midrash *Lamentations*, based on allegations that Rabbi ben Eleazar of Modi'in wants to surrender Betar, Ben Koseba summarily executes him.

9. Romans unleash artillery missiles on the southern end of the city.

10. Legionaries advance up the slope and break into the city.

11. Jewish defenders engage in street-to-street fighting. Ben Koseba is killed in the mêlée.

12. Romans slaughter the defenders of Betar. The Babylonian Talmud mentions the local streams running red with the blood of victims.

13. Betar falls to the Romans on 9 *Av* in the Jewish calendar. Prisoners are taken to Hebron and sold into slavery.

ROMAN FORCES

1. 4,500-6,000 men (2,000 men of *Legio* V *Macedonica*, 2,000 men of *Legio* XI *Claudia* and *auxilia*) under Sex. Iulius Severus

THE SIEGE OF BETAR, SUMMER AD 135

Ben Koseba stages his last stand surrounded by Iulius Severus' army.

LAST STAND AT BETAR (PP. 70–71)

In the last months of the war, Shim'on ben Koseba relocated to Betar in the Rephaim Valley. He ordered the inhabitants, refugees and his own soldiers, to hurriedly erect a stone wall with buttresses around the town. In the meantime, Roman legions V *Macedonica* and XI *Claudia* arrived and sealed off the hilltop city with a circumvallation of their own. In AD 135 – on the 9th *Av*, 4 August, according to Jewish tradition – the Roman army assaulted Betar and breached its circuit wall.

In this reconstruction of the rebel army's last stand, the Jews put up a fierce resistance. They have created a bottleneck in the street below by using an upturned cart **(1)** as a makeshift barricade, hoping to slow down the oncoming Romans, so they can be picked off by a marksman archer and spear throwers located on a verandah **(2)** of a fine, two-storey house. From rooftops and at street level, slingers **(3)** cast stones and archers loose arrows, often with little more than a buckler **(4)** each to protect them. Men of all ages and boys too attack the Romans with any weapons at their disposal. Ben Koseba's professional soldiers **(5)**, armed with captured Roman helmets, shields and swords or spears, attempt to pick off individual enemy troops at the front. However, it is clear that the repulse is already failing and the Jews have little choice now than to pull back.

Unfazed by the resistance and well practised in siege warfare, the Romans continue to advance cautiously down the main street of Betar. Behind them Jewish rebels lie dead **(6)** amidst the swirl of smoke from firebrands. Out of view, other Roman troops have entered the town, swarming the city's streets, and have broken into buildings to flush out insurgents in hiding. The target of incoming missiles, these legionaries in the vanguard of the assault have, to this point, marched in a protective *testudo* **(7)**. Approaching obstacles and sensing a trap, the centurion **(8)** has given the order to break formation and begin a charge at their disorganized opponent. They hope to capture alive rebel leader Shim'on ben Koseba and his right-hand man, the priest Eleazar. There will be rich rewards for the men who succeed.

Roman retribution for sedition is severe. No mercy will be shown on this day. Armed rebels will be hunted down and slain. Unless the Jews can stage a near miraculous recovery, the fall of Betar will mean the end of the nation of Israel and with it their King Messiah's hope for the liberation of Jerusalem.

Bar Koseba was convinced that Rabbi Eleazar wanted to surrender the city, so when the latter finished his praying, he had him brought into his presence and asked him: 'What did the Cuthean tell you?'

He answered: 'I do not know what he whispered in my ear, nor did I hear anything, because I was standing in prayer and am unaware what he said.'

Bar Koseba flew into a rage, kicked him with his foot and killed him. A heavenly voice issued forth and proclaimed: '*Woe to the worthless shepherd that leaveth the flock! The sword shall be upon his arm, and upon his right arm!*' [*Zechariah* 11:17].

It was intimated to him, 'Thou hast paralyzed the arm of Israel and blinded their right eye; therefore shall thy arm wither and thy right arm grow dim!' (Midrash Rabbah, *Lamentations* 2.2.4)

The duration of the siege of Betar is not recorded, only that 'it lasted a long time' (Eusebius, *Church History* 4.6). It would not end with a mass suicide as allegedly happened among the *sicarii* at Masada. Cut off from fresh supplies of food and water, 'the rebels were driven to final destruction by famine and thirst' (Eusebius, *Church History* 4.6). Before the final assault, the Romans would have fired missiles from ballistas and catapults into the city to break the will of the defenders to resist – probably from the higher ground of the south-western side which they occupied. The ancient Jewish texts capture something of the resilience of the rebel leader. 'He would catch the missiles from the enemy's catapults on one of his knees,' records the Midrash describing Ben Koseba's reflexes, 'and hurl them back, killing many of the foe' (Midrash Rabbah, *Lamentations* 2.2.4).

When the town was determined safe to approach the Roman troops equipped in full armour climbed up the hill. The Romans may have attacked from the south-western side (which the rebels had recently fortified), or the gates on the south-eastern side, or both simultaneously. Attacks on multiple fronts distracted the defenders and divided their resources as they tried to anticipate where the main assault would come. Archaeology offers some clues. Two badly preserved arrowheads have been found on the semi-circular buttress at the southernmost end of the town, and a pile of 22 unthrown sling stones were uncovered on top of the rectangular tower on the north-western side.

The Romans burst through the wall. A general slaughter ensued in the city's streets. The Babylonian Talmud records: 'when the enemy entered there, they pierced them with their staves, and when the enemy prevailed and captured them, they wrapped them in their scrolls and burnt them with fire' (*Gittin* 57a). As for the Prince Over Israel, 'immediately Betar was captured and Ben Koseba was killed' (Jerusalem Talmud). In this version of events his head was cut off and presented to Hadrian – a dramatic end for the man called 'Son of a Star', but most likely a fictional one since the Roman commander-in-chief was not there.

More atrocities were committed. The memory of that harrowing day has been preserved in the Jewish religious texts:

Rabbi Yohanan said: 'The brains of three hundred children were dashed upon one stone, and three hundred baskets of capsules of phylacteries were found in Bethar, each capsule having a capacity of 2130 litres.' (Midrash Rabbah, *Lamentations* 2.2.4)

Ein Gedi, Judaean Desert

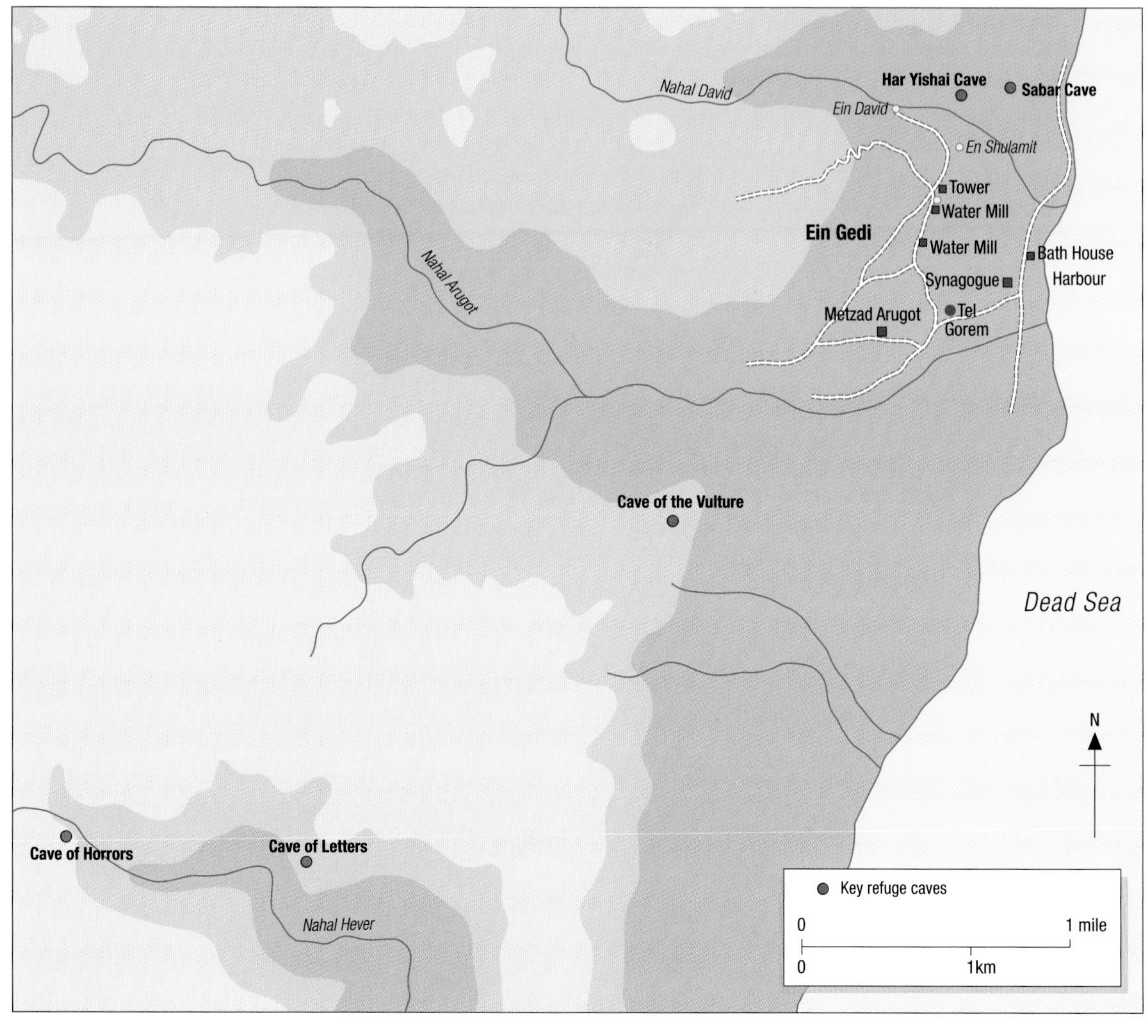

> It has been taught that Rabbi Eleazar the Great said: 'There are two streams in the valley of Yadaim, one running in one direction and one in another, and the Sages estimated that at that time they ran with two parts of water to one of blood.' (Babylonian Talmud, *Gittin* 57a)
>
> In a Baraitha [rabbinical tradition] it has been taught: 'For seven years the gentiles fertilized their vineyards with the blood of Israel without using manure.' (Babylonian Talmud, *Gittin* 57a)
>
> Rabban bar Hanah said in the name of Rabbi Yohanan: 'Forty times twenty-four phylactery boxes were found on the heads of the victims of Betar.' (Babylonian Talmud, *Gittin* 57b)

According to Jerusalem Talmud (*Ta'anit* 4:6), Betar fell on the ninth day of *Av* (*Tisha b'Av*) in the Jewish calender, or 4 August AD 135. It was the same day on which the First Temple in Jerusalem had been razed by Nebuchadnezzar II in 587 BC, and the rebuilt Second Temple was destroyed by Titus in AD 70.

CAVES OF HORROR

Mopping-up operations continued into the following year. The hobnailed Roman boot was now firmly on the bare neck of the Jewish insurgent. As the Babylonian Talmud records, the Romans now knew to look for underground hideouts: 'They were sitting in a cave and they heard a noise from above the cave and they thought that the enemies had come upon them' (*Shabbath* 60a). Some of those who had managed to flee ahead of the emperor's army had made for the apparent security of natural caves in the river valleys above Ein Gedi – in the Wadi Murabba'at, Wadi Marrazah, Nahal Arugot and Nahal Hever. Among them were Babatha and her entourage.

Many of the fugitives must have hoped that, one day, they could reemerge and return to their homes. Poignantly, among the ephemera found by archaeologists in the 1960s were front door keys. The Jews had carefully carried up to the caves all that they valued in willow baskets and wicker bags: utilitarian pots and wooden bowls, packed with the finest glassware; fishing nets and palm fibre tied with string; bronze jugs (some defaced to remove the Graeco-Roman decoration in order to make them kosher), pans and kitchen knives; sandals and brightly coloured linen fabric sheets, mantles and tunics; jewellery boxes and polished brass mirrors. They also took with them personal archives of documents on papyrus or parchment – letters (some from Ben Koseba himself), deeds, marriage contracts, receipts and biblical texts, all carefully rolled up or folded and neatly kept in pouches or wrapped and tied with string for protection. Pips, seeds, shells and stones reveal those in hiding had supplies of pomegranates, nuts, olives and dates. But this was a war zone. Arrows (some arrowheads still attached to their wooden shafts) and spears with which the Jews could defend themselves from unwelcome intruders were found with the comforts of home.

The Romans tracked them to their hideouts. Above the so-called Cave of Letters on the east side of the Nahal Hever Valley, a detachment – likely no larger than a century, and possibly from *Cohors* I *Miliaria Thracum* –

Caves are a natural feature of the Judaean Desert landscape, such as Nahal Arugot and Wadi Marrazah, near Ein Gedi. They occur when sections of the numerous limestone and sandstone layers collapse or are eroded. Though difficult to access, the caves provided readily available refuges for Jews fleeing the Roman army. (Author's collection)

The canyon of Nahal Hever drew refugees in some numbers in the last phase of the Bar Kokhba War. Discovering the caves in which they were hiding, the Roman army deployed a unit (probably *Cohors* I *Miliaria Thracum*) which built a camp on a promontory directly above the Cave of Letters and with a line of sight to the Cave of Horrors to prevent the Jews from escaping. (Author's collection)

which had once been stationed at Ein Gedi, erected a camp. They planned to be there a while. Gathering up stones the men built a defensive wall close to the edge of the cliff, and inside it installed the buildings (headquarters, food stores and ovens) necessary for a functioning military outpost. In the open spaces in between, the auxiliary soldiers set up their goatskin tents within low stone walls forming protective cubicles. A second camp across the canyon above the Cave of Horrors allowed the soldiers stationed there to message the others about movements by the insurgents.

As at Betar the Romans used thirst and starvation to do their work for them. There would be no escape for the Jews trapped below. For them, as for the Jews elsewhere in Iudaea, the Bar Kokhba War was now over:

This copper bowl has a length of palm fibre rope – complete with knots – still attached to the handle. It was found in the Cave of Letters, Nahal Hever, Judaean Desert. (Exhibit at the Israel Museum, Jerusalem. Author's collection)

Hiding from the Roman army, fighters and refugees took with them their prized personal possessions and plunder. These bronze jugs were found with other fine metal vessels, all carefully packed in a basket in the Cave of Letters, Nahal Hever. Some were intentionally defaced by removing any decoration to make them kosher. (Exhibit at the Israel Museum, Jerusalem. Author's collection)

> It happened to one group who took refuge in a cave. One of them was told: 'go and fetch a corpse of one of those killed that we may eat.' He went forth and found the body of his father and hid it and marked it, and buried it, then returned and said: 'I did not find any [corpse].' They said: 'let another go forth.' One of them went out, and followed the stench of that corpse and brought it back. They ate it and the teeth of the son became blunt. He asked: 'whence did you bring that corpse?' And was answered: 'from such and such corner.' He asked further: 'what mark was on it?' And was answered: 'such and such a mark.' He said: 'Woe to this child; he ate the flesh of his father.' (Midrash *Lamentations*).

By the winter of AD 136 the caves were silent.

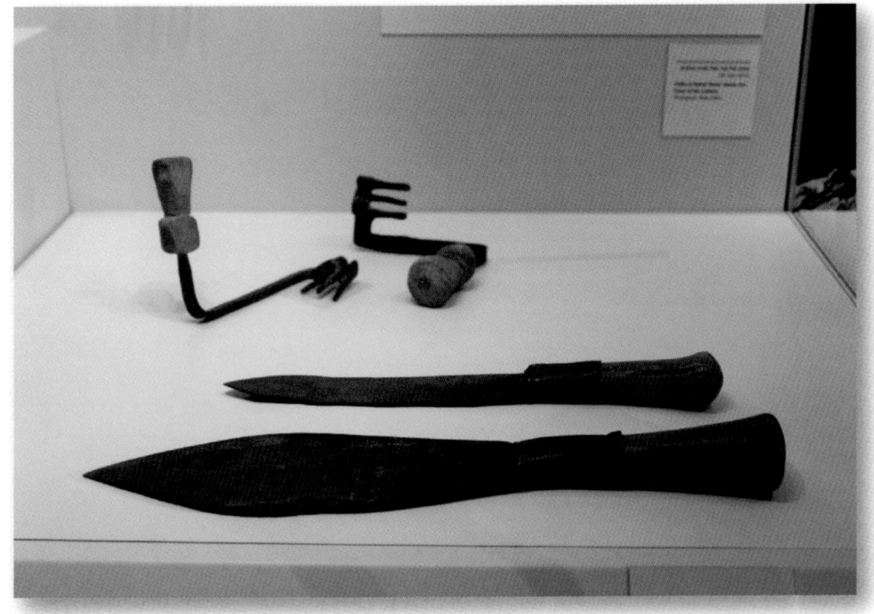

Anticipating life after the war, Jewish fighters and refugees took with them the keys to their houses, as well as their kitchen knives and other utensils, and hid them in caves in the Judaean Desert. (Exhibit at the Israel Museum, Jerusalem. Author's collection)

BLOCKADE OF THE CAVE OF LETTERS, NAHAL HEVER, AD 135/136

2

Roman auxiliary infantry (probably *Cohors* I *Miliaria Thracum*) have built a camp on a promontory directly above the Cave of Letters occupied by rebel fighters and refugees. The location also provides a line of sight to the Cave of Horrors, in which Jews hide, on the other side of the canyon. The camp is made of unhewn stones with dry joints. It features an exterior wall with a single gateway, protected by a curved wall (*clavicula*) on the exterior, enclosing an area of 1,250 square metres. Pitched within stone cubicles to shelter them from the elements, are the leather tents for the officers and soldiers. Stone ovens provide the means to bake bread, which is a staple of the soldiers' diet.

The cohort will remain here until its orders are revoked in AD 136. The fort will be found, almost intact, 18 centuries later by archaeologists assisted by the Israel Defence Forces.

1

By late AD 135, many fighters and refugees from Ein Gedi have retreated into caves in the Nahal Hever canyon. They have brought with them provisions, weapons and valuable personal belongings. On the north side of the canyon, in what will come to be known as the Cave of Letters, these effects include the legal documents of Babatha of Mehoza and military correspondence of Shim'on ben Koseba. By taking refuge in the cave, the Jews hope to wait out the final phase of the war and eventually return to their homes.

However, Roman scouts have since identified the cave as a rebel hideout. An infantry unit has been deployed to the canyon to prevent the insurrectionists from escaping or capture any that attempt to do so. The Jews, trapped inside their caves must carefully manage their supplies of food and water to survive. The Midrash, *Lamentations* describes cannibalism among the starving people.

AFTERMATH

REWARDS AND PUNISHMENTS

Some 75 years after the end of the war, Cassius Dio wrote: 'Fifty of their most important outposts and nine hundred and eighty-five of their most famous villages were razed to the ground. 580,000 men were slain in the various raids and battles, and the number of those that perished by famine, disease and fire was past finding out' (*Roman History* 69.14.1). The numbers are generally considered to be exaggerations, yet they express the large scale of the disaster that befell the rebels. Casualties were not in the hundreds or thousands, but tens or even hundreds of thousands. Yet despite their final victory, the cost in blood and treasure had been high for the Romans too. Actual numbers are not known.

The Romans' response to sedition among its subject peoples was usually severe. The punitive measures meted out to the survivors were harsh, intended to send a message to other would-be rebels. In a form of social engineering, removing troublemakers from a former conflict zone – in particular the men of military age – was a post-war policy. Having defeated the rebellious Salassi in 25 BC, the military commander A. Terrentius Varro sold some 36,000 prisoners of war into slavery. Nero Claudius Drusus had used the same approach against the Raeti in 15 BC, and his brother Tiberius Caesar had employed it after a revolt in Illyricum in 12 BC. In AD 135–136

Achieving peace (*pax*) through military victory was a central policy dictum dating back to Caesar Augustus. Hadrian's defeat of the Jewish rebels was cause for national celebration. The obverse of this silver *denarius* shows a figure (presumed to be Hadrian) wearing a tunic and helmet and holding a spear in one hand and a *victoriola* (miniature statue of winged Victory) in the other. (Roma Numismatics, www.romanumismatics.com)

Celebrating its victory over the Jews, the Roman army erected a triumphal arch near the camp of the *Legio* VI *Ferrata* at Tel Shalem. Dedicated to *imperator* Hadrian, the carved lettering on the monumental inscription is of the highest quality. The structure would have closely resembled the Arch of Titus in the Roman Forum, Rome, which was erected to mark the end of the First Jewish War. (Exhibit at the Israel Museum, Jerusalem. Author's collection)

the prisoners of the Bar Kokhba War were hauled to the annual slave market held by the Terebinth-Eloh tree in Hebron, where 'Hadrian's market' was spoken of for centuries. It was said that there were so many captives for sale that the price of a human fell to that being paid for a measure of horse feed. Unsold slaves were removed to Gaza to be auctioned there. Many others were expatriated to Egypt and elsewhere, adding great numbers to the Jewish diaspora.

Hadrian instituted a reform of regional government. Iudaea as a stand-alone province ceased to be and it was absorbed into neighbouring Syria. The combined entity was renamed, recalling an ancient name for the region coined by the Greeks: Syria-Palaestina. The two legions in the former Iudaea remained there. *Legio* V *Ferrata* now established its permanent base at Caparcotna (also known as Legio) in the Jezreel Valley along the road from Caesarea to Beth Shean in the vicinity of Megiddo. Its location gave the legion direct access to the Galilee and inland valleys of northern Palestine. Partially excavated in 2015, the fortress was some 300m by 500m (984ft by 1,640ft) and was large enough for two legions or the legion plus auxiliaries. *Legio* X *Fretensis* continued to camp at Jerusalem. Its location gave it direct access to the desert, hills and plains of the Judaean heartland. Additional auxiliary units were moved in to support them.

The weeks and months after the conclusion of the war were a time to issue rewards. Hadrian received his second acclamation after AD 136, which is believed to have been for the victory in Iudaea. It entitled him to use the form 'IMP[erator] II' on official inscriptions and coins. Hadrian was generous with decorations (*dona*) to officers and rankers for acts of valour. They were awarded to the equestrians M. Statius Priscus (*vexilla*) and Sex. Cornelius Dexter (*hasta* and *vexilla*), distinctions given for combat with the enemy. Centurion Octavius Secundus received a *corona aurea* (a crown awarded to a soldier for killing an enemy in single combat and holding the ground to the end of the battle). Centurion Sabidius Maximus received a *corona muralis* (a crown awarded to the first soldier who climbed the wall of a besieged city and successfully placed the standard of the attacking army upon it). An inscription (*CIL* XI, 3108) shows that Q. Albius Felix, centurion with *Legio* XX *Valeria Victrix* (who had likely accompanied Iulius Severus from Britannia) received the award of the *hasta pura* (a prized spear made without iron) and *corona aurea* in an unspecified Hadrianic campaign, which is presumed to be the Bar Kokhba War. A *corona aurea* was awarded to C. Nummius Constans, an *evocatus* (a veteran recalled for service).

A winged victory carrying a laurel branch is the central image on this silver *denarius* of Hadrian struck after operations in the Bar Kokhba War had ceased. The inscription proclaims 'Revered Victory'. The Roman peace in Iudaea had been won at a high cost in blood and treasure. (Roma Numismatics, www.romanumismatics.com. Coin in author's collection)

Hadrian was habitually much less generous with rewards to his direct reports. The victors of the Bar Kokhba War, however, were the exception to the rule. Triumphal ornaments (*ornamenta triumphalia*) were granted to Publicius Marcellus, Haterius Nepos and Iulius Severus. That privilege entitled them to a military parade in Rome. Not since the war to suppress the Great Illyrian Revolt (AD 6–9) had so many senators been recognized for a single campaign in this way. Each was also honoured with a bronze statue and inscribed base in his home city. Hadrian made political awards to his deputies too. Haterius Nepos, who might have suppressed a rebellion of Jews in Arabia Petraea before he joined the war effort in Iudaea, was elected suffect consul in AD 134. Lollius Urbicus became suffect consul the following year. Iulius Severus, who had successfully led the counterinsurgency, likely stayed in the region, becoming the first *legatus Augusti pro praetore* of the enlarged province of Syria-Palaestina.

A triumphal arch was erected at Tel Shalem – 12km (7½ miles) south of Beth Shean (Scythopolis) – at the location of the base of *Legio* VI *Ferrata* at the outbreak of the war. The inscription slab, which survives in fragments, measured some 10–11m (33–36ft) in length. Its exquisitely carved

After the Bar Kokhba War an amphitheatre was erected at Beit Guvrin. It may have been a reward for the Roman garrison, *Cohors* I *Miliaria Thracum*. The stone foundations supported a wooden superstructure, which could seat some 3,500 spectators. (Author's collection)

lettering – 41cm (16in.) high in the first row and 24cm (9½in.) in the second – rivals anything erected in Rome itself, including the Pantheon and Arch of Titus. It may have been constructed to mark Hadrian's visit to Iudaea in AD 130, but much more likely it celebrated the Roman victory over the Jewish rebels (following a possible but unconfirmed return by Hadrian in AD 134). It is conceivable that, understanding the significance of their victory, the three field commanders (now consuls and ex-consuls) personally lobbied for its construction.

Hadrian fulfilled his vision of a new city for army veterans. Breaking with the traditional grid pattern, the main streets of *colonia* Aelia Capitolina formed a V, emanating from the northern gate. These broad avenues lined with shops and businesses were colonnaded, affording visitors the comfort of shade from the sun in spring and summer and the rain in autumn and winter. Not one but two *fora* were established, one in the northern part of the city, the other in the western. These were large rectangular enclosures with floors of stone slabs for open air markets and conducting court hearings. The gate to the northern forum was built in the style of a triumphal arch, with a large central span, flanked by smaller arches. The jewel of the city, however, was the Temple of Jupiter Capitolinus. Where once had stood the tetrastyle Second Temple, now stood a shrine in the Greco-Roman style to the king of Olympian gods. By decree Jews were banned from entering Aelia Capitolina. To emphasize the point: 'Before its gate, that of the road by which we go to Bethlehem, he [Hadrian] set up an idol of a pig in marble, signifying the subjugation of the Jews to Roman authority' (Eusebius, *Chronicles* Hadrian's Year 20).

The rebellion had, however, been a localized affair, restricted to the Jewish heartland around Jerusalem. Jews in Galilee and Samaria had largely stayed out of the conflict. While Betar was razed and never re-occupied, the Judaean Shephelah and Judaean Hills were not laid waste by the Romans. Jewry per se was not punished; Jews were not considered an enemy of the Roman people. Judaism had a recognized status as a privileged creed (*licita religio*). Indeed, Jews even served in the Roman army. Those not representing a threat to Roman authority were permitted to remain in the former Iudaea. Thus, after the Bar Kokhba War, Jews continued to live in Lydda, the region south of the Hebron mountains and communities along the Mediterranean coast.

HERO AND MYTH

The Jews wondered how the campaign for redemption could have so completely and disastrously failed. In analysing the war two rabbinic traditions emerged for the man known as Bar Kokhba. One was of a messianic imposter. Far from being the 'Son of a Star' (*kokav*) of Rabbi Akiba's interpretation, many reflected that Shim'on ben Koseba had, instead, proved to be the 'Son of a Liar' (*kazav*). The second was of Bar Kokhba as the flawed *gibbor*. He had not proved to be a great leader in the mould of Judah Macabbee or Eleazar ben Yair, but a failure, a loser. Common to both tropes was an arrogant man. He had presumed to take the place of the real *moshiah*, and he had substituted God's divine help with a belief in his own mortal strength. There were lessons to be learned. Some sages rationalized that the Jewish people had been punished by their God for the way in which

With the war won, Hadrian proceeded to build his grand new city. The north gate of *colonia* Aelia Capitolina was a large arch for road traffic flanked by two smaller arches for pedestrians. One of these survives on the left side of the Damascus Gate, Jerusalem. As punishment for their rebellion the Jews would be banned from entering the city. (Author's collection)

they had sought national freedom. Military force was not the way to do it. Instead they must look beyond Bar Kokhba to Heaven for redemption and the means to achieve it. In time the feelings of sorrow and suffering for the loss of the dream of national freedom came to be seen as redemptive. Accepting the historical outcome of Bar Kokhba's struggle, and the shortcomings of the man, he gradually became a figure of hope and value for the future.

In the wake of tragedy Judaism itself changed. The First Jewish War resulted in the destruction of the Second Temple and redistribution of the Sanhedrin's authority to rabbis. After the Bar Kokhba War Judaism was no longer a political entity that could challenge Roman authority. Instead it was now only a religion. Its people, displaced far and wide across the Roman Empire, were even denied free access to their holiest places in Jerusalem. Rabbinic Judaism shifted to Galilee and the diaspora. The rift between Jews and Christians also widened. Followers of the messiah Christ Jesus living by the Law of Moses, who had in earlier decades been a bridge with rabbinic Jews, declined in number. Christians now trod their own separate path, becoming estranged from their Jewish brothers and sisters.

The story of Bar Kokhba became a legend embedded in Jewish tradition. According to the Midrash, *Lamentations* the 9th *Av* (4 August) was the date on which Betar fell to the Romans. It was also the date of the destruction of the First and Second Temples. On the national day of fasting held annually on *Tisha b'Av* it was customary to talk about, and reflect upon, the calamities which had befallen the Jewish people: 'When *Av* comes in gladness must be diminished' (Midrash, *Lamentations*). The occasion brought back memories of human sin, death, destruction, fire, subjugation, divine wrath and exile. It was a time for repentance.

The holiday of *Lag B'Omer*, which occurs between Pesach and Shavuot on the 18th day of the Hebrew month of *Iyyar*, took on new significance too. The day was traditionally associated with the ending of the plague, which had afflicted Rabbi Akiba's students who had gone to fight for the King Messiah. It was also the day on which Akiba's loyal disciple Rabbi Shim'on bar Yochai – a survivor of the revolt – died. On the day of his passing, the rabbi instructed his followers to mark the date as the day of his joy. He was buried at Kefar Meron. Candles were lit in his memory and festivities held there. By the 16th century, making a pilgrimage to his grave site had become popular, with bonfires, feasting, singing and dancing accompanying the event. Three centuries later children were taught about the heroism of Bar Kokhba on *Lag B'Omer*, using the day to create drawings or paper-cut decorations, and to engage in other fun outdoor activities, such as hiking, picnics, singing songs around campfires and competing in archery games and Bar Kokhba races. To generations of children the ancient war chief was presented as a much-loved folk hero, who was part of their happy memories of growing up.

What had changed? In the intervening years Bar Kokhba had become a semi-mythic character, especially in the Jewish diaspora. In 1840 Rabbi Dr. Samuel Meyer wrote a chapter in the *Israelitischer Musen-Almanach*

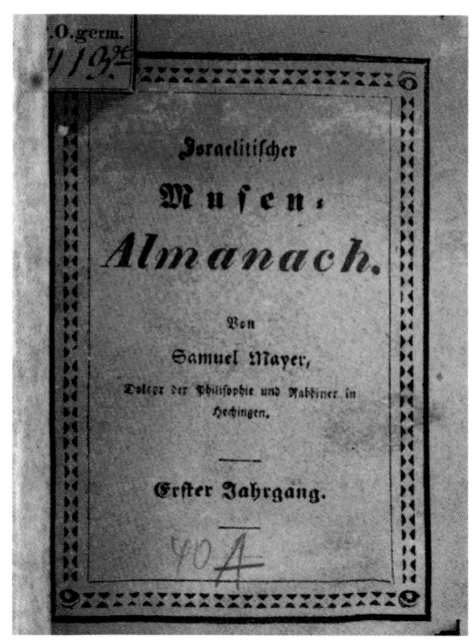

Israelitischer Musen-Almanach.

Von Samuel Mayer, Doktor der Philosophie und Rabbiner in Hechingen.

Erster Jahrgang.

IV.

Simon Barcocheba, der Messias-König.

Historische Novelle aus der ersten Hälfte des zweiten Jahrhunderts.

Im Menschenherzen gibt es viel Gedanken,
Doch nimmer wird der Rathschluß Gottes wanken.
Sprüch. Salom. 19, 21.

1. Traurig und wehmüthig schaute die Festung Bethar von der steilen Felsenmasse herab. Die Gräben und Cysternen waren aufgeschüttet und die Mauren und Wälle zerstört. Die Zeug- und Vorrathshäuser waren leer. Die Zinnen der Thürme erglänzten blutroth im Golde der flammenden Sonne. Die hohen Pforten waren nicht geschlossen und die riesigen Thore nicht gesperrt. Römische Soldaten schritten stolz durch die Gassen der weitläufigen Festungsstadt, oder sie schauten auf Trümmern in das schöne Land

In the *Israelitischer Musen-Almanach* (Almanac of the Jewish Muses) Rabbi Dr Samuel Meyer wrote a chapter entitled *Simon Barcocheba, der Messiaskönig* (*Simon Bar Kokhba, King Messiah*). Written and published in Germany in 1840, the story would be translated into many languages and spread the legend of Bar Kokhba among the Jewish diaspora. (Public domain)

(*Almanac of the Jewish Muses*) entitled *Simon Barcocheba, der Messiaskönig* (*Simon Bar Kokhba, King Messiah*). It was a telling of the story in the form of a historical novel. In it the author introduced the fantasy elements of a bow and arrow and the lion (on which, the story went, having broken out of a Roman prison, Bar Kokhba fled). A version for children was translated into many languages – French, Hungarian and Yiddish among them. Inspired by the tale, over the next one hundred years numerous works of art were produced, including dramas, operas and novels. Bar Kokhba the warrior prince became an emblematic figure printed on everything from playing cards to wall posters to dinner plates.

In the early years of the 20th century this portrayal was a source of strength for many Jews living among Europeans, who often faced anti-semitism. The racial stereotype portrayed the Jew as a coward or weakling, a person unworthy of respect. He was expected to kowtow, to take the insults and not to retaliate. Against the background of emerging nationalism among Austrians, Germans and Russians, Jewish men and women too sought to establish a national identity of their own. Under the name Bar Kokhba, people clubbed together in towns across Germany and founded associations for athletic competitions, gymnastic contests and football matches. The modern Jew was fit and healthy. This was exemplified in the bronze statue, *Bar Kokhba* (1905), by Henrik (Hanoch) Glitzenstein. This 'muscular Jew' appealed to the Zionist movement, which needed to emphasize the importance of courage and the readiness for self-sacrifice in the armed struggle for the Jewish state it was seeking to create anew in Mandatory Palestine under British administration (1920–1948).

Particularly appealing to the promoters of Zionism was the idea of Bar Kokhba as the courageous leader who refused to accept defeat. In him, David Ben-Gurion and others saw a hero to inspire young Jews who were being asked to fight to establish their homeland. (In contrast, in the 1920s the Alliance of Revisionists-Zionists in Palestine led by Ze'ev Jabotinsky named their youth movement after Betar, the hilltop stronghold where Bar Kokhba's struggle for freedom met its end.) The State of Israel was finally

Four thousand years of Jewish history come to life in Arthur Szyk's *Visual History of Israel*, completed in 1948 (the year of the foundation of the modern State of Israel) and published in 1949. The blue Star of David dominates the design. Bar Kokhba sits to the left of the Star. (The Arthur Szyk Society (www.szyk.org), CC BY-SA 4.0)

established in 1948, with Ben-Gurion as it's first prime minister. Bar Kokhba remains an important – if sometimes contentious – historical figure in Israel today because he was the last leader of a Jewish state before the rise of Zionism in modern times.

The real name of Bar Kokhba, which had since been lost in time, was finally revealed when archaeologist (and the second Chief of Staff of the Israel Defense Forces) Yigael Yadin and his team – authorized by Ben-Gurion – were exploring the refuge caves of Nahal Hever in 1961. They found handwritten letters bearing his name: Shim'on ben Koseba. The process of stripping away years of mythologizing to reveal the real man could begin. Archaeology continues to bring new finds out of the ground and into the daylight. These allow us to learn more about the Jewish rebel leader and his war.

Just two years after the end of the Bar Kokhba War, Hadrian died on 10 July AD 138. He was 62 and had ruled for almost 21 years. By then he was unpopular and 'much was said against him after his death, and by many persons' (Aelius Spartianus, *Life of Hadrian*, *Historia Augusta* 27.1). The Roman commander-in-chief remains an enigma. Famous for his wall in Britain, villa complex at Tivoli and love affair with a young man who he made a god, a few of Hadrian's letters and speeches survive as fragments – all of them official communiqués to embassies, deputies and soldiers – along with two of his verses. Nowadays Hadrian is regarded as an exemplar of Roman political and military leadership, a cultured intellectual and a civilized man. In the Jewish community, however, he is still considered a figure of cruel oppression. His name is often followed by the curse: 'may his bones be ground to dust.' He has his war with Shim'on ben Koseba to thank for it.

Bar Kokhba: Historical Memory and the Myth of Heroism, a special exhibition at the Eretz Israel Museum, Tel Aviv (20 February to 16 June 2016), presented archaeological exhibits, works of art, and numerous items attesting to the myth and popular culture that were created in Israel and in the diaspora around the hero. A highlight was the over-life-size statue *Bar Kokhba* by Henrik (Hanoch) Glitzenstein, cast in bronze in 1905. It represented a revisionist, muscular vision of the rebel leader. (Author's collection)

THE BATTLEFIELD TODAY

The epicentre of the Bar Kokhba War occurred in what is now the Judaean Shephalah and Judaean Hills in the State of Israel, and the area around Hebron and the Dead Sea in the West Bank (also known as Occupied Palestinian Territories or State of Palestine). Several sites can be visited today.

ISRAEL

Much of the hard fighting occurred at fortified villages. One example can be visited at **Horvat 'Ethri** (located within Adulam Park-France, heading south of Beit Shemesh on Highway 38, signposted on the left). Excavated by Boaz Zissu and Amirin Ganor (2009), it is now fully uncovered. Open to view are several multi-room buildings with stone walls, one of which is interpreted to be a synagogue, all arranged around a central courtyard. The site, on a hill 406m (1,320ft) above sea level, has caves carved out of the living rock. Archaeologists found harrowing evidence that the defenders were slaughtered and the settlement was razed by the Romans during their campaigning.

Scattered across the region – north and south of Beit Guvrin – are examples of caves used for hiding and storage by the Jewish insurgents. So-called **Bar Kokhba Caves** are located in the Adullam Caves Park, which

The region that was the epicentre of the Jewish revolt remains highly contentious to this day. It is now split between the State of Israel and the West Bank under the Palestinian government. Viewed from Adullam Park, the route of the modern Israeli West Bank Wall separating the two political entities is clearly delineated. (Author's collection)

The Jerusalem Archaeological Park – The Davidson Center uses multi-media interpretations to explain the archaeology of the adjacent site. It has a large collection of bricks and tiles of *Legio* X *Fretensis*. (Author's collection)

can be reached via Highway 38 (6km (2 miles) south of Ha'Ela Junction signed Churvat Madras on the left). Some of the tunnels connecting the caves are deliberately narrow, just 40cm (16in.) in places. Bringing a torch to explore the dark subterranean spaces is recommended.

After the war the victorious Roman troops were rewarded. At **Beit Guvrin** (Beit Guvrin National Park on Highway 38, on the right heading south) a stone amphitheatre, which was fully excavated in the 1990s, is now open to visitors. The 2nd-century AD structure has stone foundations and barrel vaults originally supporting a wooden superstructure for seating, able to accommodate some 3,500 spectators. The central arena features substructures used for holding wild beasts or prisoners while they waited for their grand entrance, and for storing equipment.

Hadrian's Aelia Capitolina is still preserved to an extent in the modern street plan of **Jerusalem**. The city's northern gate (now known as the **Damascus Gate**) is still a major pedestrian thoroughfare. A well-preserved arched portal – one of two for pedestrians which flanked the gate for road traffic – can be seen on the left side of the gate about 5m (16.4ft) below modern street level. The holes for its door hinges and recesses for the beams which were used to bolt the wooden door, can also be seen. Within, at Roman city level, is a museum (**Roman Square at Damascus Gate**) that explains the history of the gate using maps, photographs and illustrations.

The Roman main street (*cardo maximus*) extended from Damascus Gate in a straight line running north–south along what is now El Wad-Ha Gai Street and terminated at or around David Street. Paved with stone, it was originally flanked by roofed colonnades along its length. A section has been reconstructed in the Jewish Quarter. Crossing the ancient *cardo* was a road aligned east–west, nowadays called the Via Dolorosa. A triple arch once straddled it, which may have formed the entrance to the city's *forum*, where merchants traded goods in the open air. The large central span of it remains (now known as the **Ecce Homo Arch**), located near to the eastern end of the Via Dolorosa, while one of the smaller flanking arches is preserved in the adjacent Ecce Homo Church.

The **Davidson Center** in the **Jerusalem Archaeological Park** (Temple Mount Excavations, near the Dung Gate) explains the latest findings from the site through artefacts, interpretative videos and models. It has a collection of bricks and tiles made at the workshops of *Legio* X *Fretensis* – now located under Jerusalem's International Convention Center (Binyane Ha-Umma) – with the distinctive legionary logo of a boar and ship.

Not all of the city was repaired after the Bar Kokhba War. Stones from the upper levels of the monumental wall, which surrounded the Temple Mount and were toppled after the First Jewish War, can still be seen where they fell at the south-western corner (accessible free of charge from the street between the Western Wall Plaza and Dung Gate). This massive wall of Herodian date is best preserved at the Western or Wailing Wall. It is a place of greatest religious significance to Jews. Non-Jews can approach it (men are required to wear a skull cap or *kippah*, which is available at the site). A visit at night when the plaza is floodlit is a memorable experience. Nothing remains of the Temple of Jupiter Capitolinus, which is assumed to have stood on the site now occupied by the Dome of the Rock (the shrine sacred to Muslims).

The spectacular **Israel Museum and Shrine of the Book** (Derech Ruppin 11, opposite the Knesset) houses an extensive collection of Bar Kokhba War relics. It includes surviving letters of Ben Koseba, the documents of Babatha, keys, baskets, Jewish religious artefacts, coins overstruck by the revolutionary administration, as well as arrows and other weapons recovered from various caves near Ein Gedi. The remains of the exquisite bronze statue of the Emperor Hadrian, which likely came from a temporary camp of *Legio* VI *Ferrata* at Tel Shalem, and dated to around AD 130–132, is the centrepiece of the newly refurbished gallery. Adjacent cases display fragments of Roman arms and armour of the period, including the complete legionary helmet with cross-braces often assumed to come from Hebron, but which is, in fact, of unknown provenance. Examples of bricks and tiles made by *Legio* X, some with imprints of the soles of Roman boots, are on display. Also on view are the fragments of the Roman inscriptions from the triumphal arch at Tel Shalem and from the Damascus Gate in Jerusalem of *Legio* X *Fretensis* (a second piece of the slab can be seen at **Archaeological Museum-Studium Biblicum Franciscanum** in Jerusalem).

As for the protagonists, the giant bronze **Knesset Menorah** – standing at the edge of Gan Havradim (Rose Garden) opposite the Knesset building – shows Shim'on ben Koseba on an inner branch (opposite King David). On the helmet of the stylized figure depicted in his moment of death is a relief of a lion, after the myth that he would ride to battle on one. It was designed by Benno Elkan (1877–1960). The **Tomb of Rabbi Akiba** is at Tiberias, located on the mountainside behind the Kiryat Moshe neighborhood, overlooking the town and the Sea of Galilee. It has been a place of pilgrimage since the early Middle Ages.

WEST BANK

The great hilltop fortress of **Herodium** (in Herodion National Park) is located 12km (7 miles) south of Jerusalem and 5km (3 miles) south-east of Bethlehem off Highway 398. Built by Herod the Great it was occupied by men loyal to Ben Koseba – and by the rebel leader himself – in the early years of the War. Cut into the hillside are tunnels dug by troops during the First Jewish War and extended by Ben Koseba's men.

Betar, the site of Ben Koseba's last stand, is generally believed to be Khirbet el-Yahud (Arabic meaning 'Ruin of the Jews') beside the modern village of Battir (or Bittir). Located behind the 1949 Armistice Agreement Line (the so-called Green Line), it is accessible via Bethlehem. There is now little to see of the ancient citadel explored by W.D. Carroll (1923–24) and David Ussishkin (1993). Much of the archaeology has either been disturbed or destroyed, but a section of wall and a circular buttress are exposed. From within Israel Betar can be seen at a distance from Mount Tayasim Nature Reserve (near the Israeli Airmen Memorial) south-east of Jerusalem off Highway 395 to Beit Shemesh. Viewed on the far horizon its close proximity to the Holy City and the difficulty of the terrain to an invading army can be fully appreciated.

Some of the caves in which Jews hid themselves with their personal belongings are located near **Ein Gedi** on the western shore of the Dead Sea, some 80km (50 miles) south-east of Jerusalem, reached on Highway 90. Caves, examples of which can be seen at the Ein Gedi Nature Reserve encompassing the river valleys of the rivers Nahal David and Nahal Arugot, occur naturally in the local geology. About 5km (3 miles) south-west of Ein Gedi on the north side of the adjacent valley of Nahal Hever are the entrances to the so-called Cave of Letters (Ma'arat Ha'Igrot), which merge into a single 150m-long (492ft) cavern inside. Explored in the 1960s by Yigael Yadin (1971), here was found an archive of the residents of Ein Gedi, which included a packet of 15 letters of Ben Koseba as well as the personal documents of Babatha Bat Shim'on. The remains of the small Roman siege fort, the garrison of which watched for people trying to escape from the cave, is located above. A low wall of loose stones encloses a triangle-shaped space (unlike the forts at Masada) with bases of rectangular structures for tents, traces of ovens and other elements of military camp life.

The Israel Museum in Jerusalem has displays of important artefacts from the Bar Kokhba War period. It also presents occasional special archaeological exhibitions, such as *Hadrian: An Emperor Cast in Bronze* (22 December 2015 to 27 June 2016). It brought together bronze portraits of Hadrian from the British Museum, London, the Louvre, Paris and Tel Shalem, Israel for the first time. (Author's collection)

Farther up the valley on the other side is the Cave of Horrors (Ma'arat Ha'Eimim), so named on account of the several skulls and skeletons discovered there. Above it is a monument (the unveiling of which, at a ceremony attended by then Prime Minister Menachem Begin, was highly controversial). Its inscription, translated from Hebrew, reads: 'Here lie the bones of the warriors of Bar Kokhba who fought the Romans in the Iudean desert during AD 132–135, them and their families. The bones were collected in the Cave of Letters and the Cave of Horrors and buried in a ceremony (11.5.1982)'. (It was vandalized in 2005, but reconstructed three years later.) Some believe the bones were actually those of Roman troops.

BIBLIOGRAPHY

Alexander, Paul J., 'Letters and Speeches of the Emperor Hadrian', *Harvard Studies in Classical Philology* 49 (1938), pp. 141–177

Avi-Yonah, M., 'The Development of the Roman Road System in Palestine', *Israel Exploration Journal* 1.1 (1950–1951), pp. 54–60

Baker, Renan, 'Epiphanius, "On Weights and Measures" §14: Hadrian's Journey to the East and the Rebuilding of Jerusalem', *Zeitschrift für Papyrologie und Epigraphik* 182 (2012), pp. 157–167 Bentwich, Norman, 'The Graeco-Roman View of Jews and Judaism in the Second Century', *The Jewish Quarterly Review* 23.4 (Apr. 1933), pp. 337–348

Ben-Zeev, Miriam Pucci, 'L. Tettius Crescens' *expeditio Iudaeae*', *Zeitschrift für Papyrologie und Epigraphik* 133 (2000), pp. 256–258

Birley, Anthony R., *Hadrian: The Restless Emperor* (Roman Imperial Biographies), Routledge (2000)

Bowersock, Glenn W., 'A Roman Perspective on the Bar Kokhba War' in: Green, William S. (ed.), *Approaches to Ancient Judaism* Vol. 2, Scholars Press (1980), pp. 131–141.

Broshi, Magen, 'Agriculture and Economy in Roman Palestine: Seven Notes on the Babatha Archive', *Israel Exploration Journal* 42.3/4 (1992), pp. 230–240

Bruun, Christer, 'The Spurious "Expeditio Ivdaeae" under Trajan', *Zeitschrift für Papyrologie und Epigraphik* 93 (1992), pp. 99–106

Bryce, Trevor, *Ancient Syria: A Three Thousand Year History*, Oxford University Press (2014)

Carroll, W.D., 'Bittîr and Its Archaeological Remains', *The Annual of the American Schools of Oriental Research* 5 (1923–1924), pp. 77–103

Clermont-Ganneau, Charles, *Archaeological Researches in Palestine during the Years* 1873–1874, Volume 1, Palestine Exploration Fund, London (1899)

Cotton, Hannah M. and Eck, Werner, 'P. Murabba'at 114 und die Anwesenheit römischer Truppen in den Höhlen des Wadi Murabba'at nach dem Bar Kochba Aufstand', *Zeitschrift für Papyrologie und Epigraphik* 138 (2002), pp. 173–183

D'Amato, Raffaele and Sumner, Graham, *Arms and Armour of the Imperial Roman Soldier: From Marius to Commodus, 112 BC–AD 192*, Frontline (2009)

Dabrowa, E., *The Governors of Roman Syria from Augustus to Septimius Severus*, Bonn, Habelt (1998)

Davies, R.W., 'Fronto, Hadrian and the Roman Army', *Latomus* 27.1 (Janvier–Mars 1968), pp. 75–95

Davies, R.W., Cohors I Hispanorum and the Garrisons of Maryport, read at Temple Sowerby, 8 July 1977 (http://archaeologydataservice.ac.uk/archiveDS/archiveDownload?t=arch-2055-1/dissemination/pdf/Article_Level_Pdf/tcwaas/002/1977/vol77/tcwaas_002_1977_vol77_0004.pdf, accessed 27 February 2017)

Deutsch, Robert, 'A Lead Weight of Hadrian: The Prototype for the Bar Kokhba Weights', *Israel Numismatic Journal* 14 (2000–2002), pp. 125–128

Deutsch, Robert, 'A Lead Weight of Shimon Bar Kokhba', *Israel Exploration Journal* 51.1 (2001), pp. 96–98

Dorsey. D., *The Roads and Highways of Ancient Israel*, Johns Hopkins University Press (1991)

Eck, Werner, 'The bar Kokhba Revolt: The Roman Point of View', *The Journal of Roman Studies* 89 (1999), pp. 76–89

Eliav, Yaron Z., 'Hadrian's Actions in the Jerusalem Temple Mount According to Cassius Dio and Xiphilini Manus', *Jewish Studies Quarterly* 4.2 (1997), pp. 125–144

Eschel, Hanan, 'A Coin of Bar Kokhba from a Cave in Wadi el-Mackuck', *Israel Numismatic Journal* 9 (1987), pp. 51–52

Eshel, H., 'The History of Research and Survey of the Finds of the Refuge Cave', in: Eshel, H., and Amit, D., *The Bar-Kokhba Refuge Caves* (1998), pp. 60–61 (Hebrew)

Eschel, Hanan, 'The Bar Kochba Revolt, 132–135', in: Katz, Steven T. (ed.), *The Cambridge History of Judaism*, IV. *The Late Roman Period*, Cambridge University Press (2006), pp. 105–127

Eschel, Hanan, '"Bethar was captured and the city was plowed": Jerusalem, Aelia Capitolina and the Bar Kokhba Revolt', *Eretz-Israel: Archaeological, Historical and Geographical Studies*, Teddy Kollek Volume (2007), pp. 21–28

Eschel, Hanan, and Amit, David, 'A Tetradrachm of Bar Kokhba from a Cave in Nahal Hever', *Israel Numismatic Journal* 11 (1991), pp. 33–35

Eshel H. and Zissu B., 'Roman Coins from the "Cave of the Sandal" West of Jericho', *Israel Numismatic Journal* 13 (1999), pp. 70–77

Eshel, Hanan, and Zissu, Boaz, *The Bar Kokhba Revolt – An Archaeological Perspective*. Jerusalem, Yad Ben Zvi (2015) (Hebrew)

Eshel, Hanan, Zissu, Boaz, and Barkay, Gabriel, 'Sixteen Bar Kokhba Coins from Roman Sites in Europe', in: Barag, D., and Zissu, B. (eds.), *Studies in Honour of Arnold Spaer* [*Israel Numismatic Journal* 17] (2010), pp. 91–97

Garrett, M.G., 'Thracian Units in the Roman Army', *Israel Exploration Journal* 19.4 (1969), pp. 215–224

Gergel, Richard A., 'The Tel Shalem Hadrian Reconsidered', *American Journal of Archaeology* 95.2 (Apr. 1991), pp. 231–251

Geva, Hillel, 'The Camp of the Tenth Legion in Jerusalem: An Archaeological Reconsideration', *Israel Exploration Journal* 34.4 (1984), pp. 239–254

Gichon, Mordechai, 'New Insight into the Bar Kokhba War and a Reappraisal of Dio Cassius 69.12–13', *The Jewish Quarterly Review* 77.1 (July 1986), pp. 15–43

Gichon, Mordechai, and Vitale, Michaela, 'Arrow-Heads from Ḥorvat 'Eqed', *Israel Exploration Journal* 41.4 (1991), pp. 242–257

Golan, David, 'Hadrian's Decision to supplant "Jerusalem" by "Aelia Capitolina"', *Historia: Zeitschrift für Alte Geschichte* 35.2 (2nd Qtr. 1986), pp. 226–239

Goodman, Martin, 'Trajan and the Origins of Roman Hostility to the Jews', *Past & Present* 182 (Feb. 2004), pp. 3–29

Grant, Michael, *The Jews in the Roman World*, Barnes and Noble (reprint, 1995)

Gray, William D., 'The Founding of Aelia Capitolina and the Chronology of the Jewish War under Hadrian', *The American Journal of Semitic Languages and Literatures* 39.4 (July 1923), pp. 248–256.

Gruber, Daniel, *Rabbi Akiba's Messiah: The Origins of Rabbinic Authority*, Elijah Publishing (1999)

Hadas, Gideon, 'Where was the Harbour of 'En-Gedi Situated?', *Israel Exploration Journal* 43.1 (1993), pp. 45–49

Hadas, Israel Gideon, Liphschitz, Nili, and Bonani, Georges, 'Two Ancient Wooden Anchors from Ein Gedi, on the Dead Sea', *International Journal of Nautical Archaeology* 34.2 (Oct. 2005), pp. 299–307

Harel, M., 'Israelite and Roman Roads in the Iudean Desert', *Israel Exploration Journal* 17.1 (1967), pp. 18–26

Heichelheim, F.M., 'New Light on the End of Bar Kokba's War', *The Jewish Quarterly Review, New Series* 34.1 (Jul. 1943), pp. 61–63

Hendin, David, 'On the Identity of Eleazar the Priest', *Israel Numismatic Journal* 18 (2014), pp. 155–167

Horbury, William, *Jewish War under Trajan and Hadrian*, Cambridge University Press (2014)

Hufer, Holger, *Der Bar Kochba-Aufstand (132-135/36 n. Chr.): Ursachen, Verlauf und Folgen unter Einbeziehung aktueller wissenschaftlicher Erkenntnisse*, Grin Verlag (2013)

Hufer, Holger, *Die Erhebung der Juden unter Bar Kochba: Der heroische Kampf des jüdischen Volkes gegen die römische Besatzung im 2. Jhd. n. Chr*, Diplomica (2014)

Isaac, Benjamin, and Roll, Israel, 'Legio II Traiana in Judaea: A Reply', *Zeitschrift für Papyrologie und Epigraphik* 47 (1982), pp. 131–132

Isaac, Benjamin, and Roll, Israel, *Roman Roads in Judaea I: The Legio-Scythopolis Road*, BAR International Series 141, Oxford (1982)

Jacobson, David M. and Kokkinos, Nikos, *Judaea and Rome in Coins, 65 BCE–135 CE*, Spink (2012)

Kanael, B., 'Notes on the Dates Used During The Bar Kokhba Revolt', *Israel Exploration Journal* 21.1 (1971), pp. 39–46

Kennedy, D.L., 'Legio VI Ferrata: The Annexation and Early Garrison of Arabia', *Harvard Studies in Classical Philology* 84 (1980), pp. 283–309
Kislev, M.E., 'Vegetal food of Bar Kokhba rebels at Abi'or Cave near Jericho', *Review of Palaeobotany and Palynology* 73 1–4 (30 September 1992), pp. 153–160
Klein, E., Zissu, B., Goldenberg, G., and Ganor, A., 'New Studies on the Hideouts Complexes in the Iudean Foothills', in: Stiebel, G.D., Peleg-Barkat, O., Ben-Ami, D., and Gadot, Y. (eds.), *New Studies in the Archaeology of Jerusalem and its Region, Collected Papers, Vol. IX*, Jerusalem (2015), pp. 235–255 (Hebrew)
Kloner, Amos, 'Underground Hiding Complexes from the Bar Kokhba War in the Iudean Shephelah', *The Biblical Archaeologist* 46.4 (Dec. 1983), pp. 210–221
Kloner A., and Zissu B., 'Underground Hiding Complexes in Israel and the Bar Kokhba Revolt', *Opera Ipogea* 1 (2009), pp. 9–28
Kloner A., and Zissu B., 'The Geographical Distribution of Hiding Complexes and Refuge Caves during the Bar Kokhba Revolt – Some New Insights' in: Tavger, A., Amar, Z., and Billig, M., (eds.), *Highland's Depth, Ephraim Range and Binyamin Research Studies* 4, Ariel-Talmon (2014), pp. 57–68 (Hebrew)
Laperrousaz, E.M., 'L'Hérodium, quartier général de Bar Kokhba?', *Syria* 41.3/4 (1964), pp. 347–358
Lapin, H., 'Palm Fronds and Citrons: Notes on Two Letters from Bar Kosiba's Administration', *Hebrew Union College Annual* 64 (1993), pp. 111–135
Mantel, Hugo, 'The Causes of the Bar Kokba Revolt', *The Jewish Quarterly Review* 58.3, (Jan. 1968), pp. 224–242
Mantel, Hugo, 'The Causes of the Bar Kokba Revolt (Continued)', *The Jewish Quarterly Review* 58.4 (Apr. 1968), pp. 274–296
Marks, Richard G., *The Image of Bar Kokhba in Traditional Jewish Literature: False Messiah and National Hero* (Hermeneutics: Studies in the History of Religions), Penn State University Press (2005)
Maxfield, Valerie, *The Military Decorations of the Roman Army*, Batsford (1981)
Menashe, Har-el, 'The Route of Salt, Sugar and Balsam Caravans in the Judaean Desert', *GeoJournal* 2.6, Geography in Israel (1978), pp. 549–556
Meshorer, Y., *The Coinage of Aelia Capitolina*, Jerusalem (1989) (Hebrew)
Mildenberg, Leo, 'Bar Kokhba Coins and Documents', *Harvard Studies in Classical Philology* 84 (1980), pp. 311–335
Mildenberg, Leo, *The Coinage of the Bar Kokba War, Typos VI*, Sauerländer (1984)
Mor, Menachem, 'Two Legions: The Same Fate? (The Disappearance of the Legions IX *Hispana* and XXII *Deiotariana*)', *Zeitschrift für Papyrologie und Epigraphik* 62 (1986), pp. 267–278
Mor, Menachem, 'Are there any New Factors Concerning the Bar-Kokhba Revolt?', *Studia Antiqua et Archaeologica* 18 (2012), pp. 161–193
Mor, Menachem, 'What does Tel Shalem have to do with the Bar Kokhba Revolt?', *Scripta Judaica Cracoviensa* 11 (2013), pp. 79–96
Mor, Menachem, *The Second Jewish War: The Bar Kokhba War, 132–136 CE*, (The Brill Reference Library of Judaism Vol. 50), Leiden: Brill (2016)
Netzer, Ehud, 'Jewish Rebels Dig Strategic Tunnel System', *Biblical Archaeology Review* 14, 4 (1988)
Netzer, Ehud, and Arzi S., 'Herodium Tunnels', *Qadmoniot* 18, (1985), pp. 33–38 (Hebrew)
Opper, Thorsten, *The Emperor Hadrian: Empire and Conflict*, British Museum (2008)
Perowne, Stewart H., *Hadrian*, Croom Helm (reprint 1986)
Porat, Roi, Eschel, Hanan, and Frumkin, Amos, 'Finds from the Bar Kokhba Revolt from Two Caves at En Gedi', *Palestine Exploration Quarterly*, 139.1 (2007), pp. 35–53
Porat, Roi, Eshel, Hanan, and Frumkin, Amos, 'The "Caves of the Spear": Refuge Caves from the Bar-Kokhba Revolt North of ʿEn-Gedi', *Israel Exploration Journal* 59.1 (2009), pp. 21–46
Rea, J.R., 'The Legio II Traiana in Judaea?', *Zeitschrift für Papyrologie und Epigraphik* 38 (1980), pp. 220–221
Roll, Y., 'The Roman Road Network in Eretz-Israel', *Qadmoniot* IX (1976), pp. 38–50 (Hebrew)
Schäfer, Peter, *Bar Kokhba War Reconsidered: New Perspectives on the Second Jewish Revolt Against Rome, Texts and Studies in Ancient Judaism, 100*, Mohr Siebeck (2003)
Schiffman, Lawrence H., 'Jerusalem: Twice Destroyed, Twice Rebuilt', *The Classical World* 97.1 (Autumn 2003), pp. 31–40
Schoenfeld, Andrew J., 'Sons of Israel in Caesar's Service: Jewish Soldiers in the Roman Military', *Shofar: An Interdisciplinary Journal of Jewish Studies* 24.3 (Spring 2006), pp. 115–126
Sidebottom, Harry, 'The Army in Syria', *The Classical Review* 53.2 (Oct. 2003), pp. 431–433

Stebnicka, Krystyna, *Identity of the Diaspora: Jews in Asia Minor in the Imperial Period*, Journal of Juristic Papyrology (2015)

Stiebel, Guy D., 'Military Equipment', in: Syon, Danny (ed.), *Gamla III: The Shmarya Gutmann Excavations 1976–1989: Finds and Studies. Part 1*, Israel Antiquities Authority Report 56 (2014), pp. 57–108

Stinespring, William F., 'Hadrian in Palestine, 129/130 A. D.', *Journal of the American Oriental Society* 59.3 (Sep. 1939), pp. 360–365

Tsafrir, Yoram, and Zissu, Boaz, 'A Hiding Complex of the Second Temple Period and the Time of the Bar-Kokhba Revolt at 'Ain-'Arrub in the Hebron Hills', *Journal of Archaeology* Supplementary Series 49 The Roman and Byzantine Near East Vol. 3 (2002), pp. 7–36

Turel, Sara (ed.), *Bar Kokhba: Historical Memory and the Myth of Heroism*, Eretz Israel Museum Tel Aviv (2016)

Ussishkin, David, 'Archaeological Soundings at Betar, Bar-Kochba's Last Stronghold', *Tel Aviv* 20 (1993), pp. 66–97

Wise, Michael Owen, *Language and Literacy in Roman Judaea: A Study of the Bar Kokhba Documents (The Anchor Yale Bible Reference Library)*, Yale (2015)

Yadin, Y., 'Expedition D', *Israel Exploration Journal* 11.1/2, The Expedition to the Judaean Desert 1960 (1961), pp. 36–52

Yadin, Yigael, *Bar-Kokhba: The Rediscovery of the Legendary Hero of the Last Jewish Revolt Against Imperial Rome*, Random House (1971)

Yadin, Yadin et al., *The Documents from the Bar-Kokhba Period in the Cave of Letters. Hebrew, Aramaic and Nabatean-Aramaic Papyri*, Israel Exploration Society, Israel, 1989–2002

Zeitlin, Solomon, 'Bar Kokba and Bar Kozeba', *The Jewish Quarterly Review* 43.1 (Jul. 1952), pp. 77–82

Zissu, B., and Eshel, H., 'Coins and Hoards from the Time of the Bar Kokhba Revolt', *Hoards and Genizot as Chapters in History* [Hecht Museum Catalogue no. 33], Haifa (2013), pp. 31–39

Zissu, Boaz, and Ecker, Avner, 'A Roman Military Fort North of Bet Guvrin/ Eleutheropolis?', *Zeitschrift für Papyrologie und Epigraphik* 188 (2014), pp. 293–312Zissu, Boaz, and Ganor, Amir, 'A Lead Weight of Bar Kokhba's Administration', *Israel Exploration Journal* 56.2 (2006), pp. 178–182

Zissu, Boaz, and Ganor, Amir, 'Horvat 'Ethri – a Jewish village from the Second Temple period and the Bar Kokhba Revolt in the Iudean foothills', *Journal of Jewish Studies* 60.1 (2009), pp. 90–136

Zissu, B., Klein, E., and Kloner, A., 'Settlement Processes in the Territorium of Roman Jerusalem (Aelia Capitolina)', in: Alvarez, J.M., Nogales, T., and Roda, I. (eds.), *XVIII CIAC: Centre and Periphery in the Ancient World*, Merida (2014), pp. 219–223

Zissu, Boaz, Eshel, Hanan, Langford, Boaz, and Frumkin, Amos, 'Coins from the Bar Kokhba Revolt Hidden in Me'arat Ha-Te'omim (Mŭghâret Umm et Tûeimîn), Western Jerusalem Hills', *Israeli Numismatic Journal* 17 (2010), pp. 113–147

Zissu, Boaz, Porat, Ro'i, Langford, Boaz, and Frumkin, Amos, 'Archaeological remains of the Bar Kokhba Revolt in the Te'omim Cave', *Journal of Jewish Studies* 62.2 (2011), pp. 262–283

INDEX

References to illustrations are in **bold**